**Illustrator:**
Agi Palinay

**Editor:**
Janet Cain, M. Ed.

**Editorial Project Manager:**
Ina Massler Levin, M.A.

**Editor in Chief:**
Sharon Coan, M.S. Ed.

**Art Director:**
Elayne Roberts

**Associate Designer:**
Denise Bauer

**Cover Artist:**
Sue Fullam

**Product Manager:**
Phil Garcia

**Imaging:**
Alfred Lau
James Edward Grace

**Publishers:**
Rachelle Cracchiolo, M.S. Ed.
Mary Dupuy Smith, M.S. Ed.

## Learning Center Activities

# Holidays

## K-2

**Author:**
*Susie Alexander*

***Teacher Created Materials, Inc.***
P.O. Box 1040
Huntington Beach, CA 92647
**ISBN-1-57690-074-6**

# Table of Contents

**Introduction** . . . 3
How to Set Up the Center . . . 3
How to Use the Center . . . 5
How to Use This Book . . . 6

**Center Management** . . . 7
Holiday Calendar . . . 7
Center Rules . . . 8
Holiday Center Sign . . . 9
Holiday Clip Art . . . 10

**Holidays and Activities** . . . 13
*Labor Day* . . . 13
Job Hats
*Halloween* . . . 16
Masquerade Mask—Halloween Word Games—Pumpkin Pattern
*Thanksgiving* . . . 21
Cornucopia Pattern—Cornucopia Food Cards—Native American Pictographs
*Hanukkah* . . . 27
Dreidel Pattern—The Dreidel Game—Making Latkes
*Christmas* . . . 32
Lift the Gift—Christmas Wrap Around the World—Christmas Poet-Tree—Christmas Poet-Tree Word Cards—Christmas Gift List
*Kwanzaa* . . . 40
Kwanzaa Mat—Traditional African Clothing—Paper Dolls
*New Year's* . . . 44
Baby New Year's New Beginnings—Father Time's Contractions
*Martin Luther King, Jr. Day* . . . 47
"I Have a Dream" Mobile—Martin Luther King, Jr. Puzzle
*Valentine's Day* . . . 51
Conversation Hearts Graph—Pencil Toppers—Broken Hearts Compound Words
*Saint Patrick's Day* . . . 56
Leprechaun Hand Puppet—Leprechaun Maze
*Easter* . . . 60
Jelly Bean Cards—Ukrainian Egg Designs
*Earth Day* . . . 64
*Mother's Day* . . . 66
Mom's Mini-Book
*Father's Day* . . . 68
Tie Patterns—Dad Word Strip—Dad's Doings

**Patriotic/National Holidays** . . . 72
*Columbus Day, Election Day, Veterans Day, Presidents' Day, Cinco de Mayo, Memorial Day, Flag Day, Canada Day, Independence Day*
Be an Explorer—Buttons and Medals—Do You Know Your Presidents?—Money Matching—Spanish Words—"My Country 'Tis of Thee"

 

# Introduction

Holidays are times of fun and celebration. Learning about holidays helps students recognize and appreciate cultural similarities and diversity. *Learning Center Activities: Holidays* has been organized to help busy teachers implement activities related to celebrations that take place throughout the year. Its 80 exciting pages are filled with a wide variety of lesson ideas and activities designed for use with primary students. The holiday theme is connected across the curriculum with projects that allow for different learning styles. These activities can be used as independent assignments or to encourage cooperative learning.

Ever increasing in popularity, the learning center is a perfect way for students to experience learning activities. The time spent using the center is an alternative to traditional seat work. Students are responsible for managing their time, completing the center activities, and putting away the materials they use. The center activities are prepared in advance. As students work at the center, teachers have more time to circulate around the classroom providing additional learning opportunities.

Learning centers can and should be more than just a place for students to do art projects when their seat work is complete. While exploring holidays, students working in the holiday learning center will also be developing motor skills, critical thinking skills, and a variety of academic skills. Students will have so much fun they may not realize that they are learning!

# How to Set Up the Center

This book has been designed to help teachers easily prepare a learning center for holidays. You may wish to create the activities before the school year starts.

### Display

It is best if the table you use for the center can be pushed up against a wall under a bulletin board. If that is not possible, you can make a display board that will be used for hanging signs and sample projects. Use the following directions to create a display board: cut off the top, bottom, and one side of a large cardboard box. This will leave you with three sides of the box. Paint the cardboard red or green, since these colors go with most holidays. Allow the paint to dry. Attach Velcro pieces to the display board so that the center signs can be posted. If you are using a bulletin board, staples or thumbtacks can be used.

### Signs

For each holiday in this book, reproduce the center sign (page 9) on heavy paper, like card stock or tagboard. Add the appropriate clip art (pages 10-12) to decorate each sign. Color or paint the sign if desired. Then laminate it for durability. Create a sign showing the name of each holiday, using white tagboard. After you write the name of the holiday in bold letters, cut, color, and glue the clip art or pictures from magazines to the signs in any creative way. Save time by making all of the signs at once and filing them into a file box (page 4).

# How to Set Up the Center *(cont.)*

### *Materials Set-Up*

Arrange your center with a table and up to four chairs, against a wall with a bulletin board or with a display board (page 3). Under the table, place a trash can and file box with all of the year's holiday materials. On top of the table, arrange the supply baskets, project materials, a cassette player with headphones, holiday-themed puzzles, and appropriate literature or technology resources. Leave most of the table bare, so students have room to complete the learning activities.

### *Other Decorations*

What is a holiday without decorations? To make your Holiday Center more festive, add one or two simple decorations that are distinctive to that celebration. Some examples include a Christmas garland or Christmas tree lights, an Easter basket complete with cellophane grass and plastic eggs, and a jack-o'-lantern for Halloween. Each holiday, students will enjoy knowing they have something different to look forward to in their favorite center.

### *Supply Baskets*

A permanent fixture in the center is a supply basket containing pencils, colored markers, crayons, children's scissors, glue, and glue sticks. There need only be enough supplies for up to four students. Provide a basket or a box lid with scratch paper for students to use when solving some of the games and puzzles.

### *Surprise Box*

A fun tactile, critical-thinking skills activity is exploring the surprise box—a special container in which students can feel and/or hear an item but not see it. After feeling and guessing what the object might be, they are able to pull it out and check their guesses. Make a surprise box that will contain new seasonal items for each holiday using the following directions: Wrap white contact paper around an empty oatmeal (cylinder-shaped) container. Cut off the toe of a clean, old white sock. Slip the other end of the sock over the opening of the container. Tape the sock on to the container so it does not slip off. Decorate the container with holiday stickers, or use the clip art (pages 10-12). Each holiday lesson suggests a few items that you can put in the surprise box. Be sure to place the items in the box one at a time and change them frequently. This will help maintain the element of surprise.

### *File Box*

The file box is central to your Holiday Center's organization. It needs to contain hanging file folders (one for each holiday) and smaller manila file folders (one for each activity). For instance, there will be a hanging file folder for Thanksgiving that will include separate manila folders for these activities: Let's Talk Turkey, Food Sorting, and Native American Pictographs. Any other activities you create for each holiday can easily be added to this system. Rotate the hanging files so that the current holiday is always in the front.

 

# How to Use the Center

Students will need only minimal initial instruction in how to use the center. At the beginning of the school year, you should introduce the Holiday Center and explain the file box system. Each student will pull out a folder from the current holiday and work on the project independently.

Each time you introduce a new holiday to the center, you will want to take a few minutes to mention the activities in the folder for that particular holiday. This will be especially helpful for non-readers, who would find written directions difficult to follow. You will also find that it helps to motivate students to do the center activities.

You may wish to organize the use of the centers so that groups of students get to visit them on a weekly or semi-weekly basis. If you have more than one center in your classroom, you will want to schedule center time. A 20-minute block of time should be enough for students to accomplish one or more of the Holiday Center activities. Students who are not at the centers could be engaged in a variety of activities such as cooperative learning groups or silent reading time. Schedule some groups to go to the centers while you are working with others.

As an alternative to scheduling the use of centers by groups, you can do it individually using a craft stick system. Write each student's name on a craft stick. Before students use the center their craft sticks are placed in a cup labeled "WANT TO." After students use the center, their craft sticks are placed in a cup labeled "BEEN THERE — DONE THAT." Students can use the center as often as they like, but if someone wants to use the center whose stick is in the "WANT TO" cup, he or she has priority. Using this system, all of the craft sticks should be placed in the "WANT TO" cup each time a new holiday is introduced. A calendar (page 7) has been provided to help you plan when to study each holiday. Use it only as a general guideline, since the dates for many holidays change from year to year.

When you introduce the Holiday Center at the beginning of the year, you will need to describe the kind of behavior you expect from students. Appropriate behavior at the center is especially important since you will most often be leading other activities. Some students will be working on independent tasks or group projects, and they cannot be distracted by students doing a center activity. Therefore, out of respect for the teacher and other students, groups or individuals using the center must follow the rules. The rules (page 8) should be reproduced on brightly colored construction paper, laminated, and permanently posted in the center.

A student who is not able to handle the responsibility of working in the center independently or with a cooperative learning group should lose the privilege of participating in the activities. You may wish to initiate a warning system before denying students the opportunity to use the center. For example, if a student receives two warnings, he or she would not be allowed to use the center for the next holiday. Rewarding those students with particularly good behavior by giving them extra time at the center is a good motivator for all students.

# How to Use This Book

This book lists holiday activities in chronological order, beginning and ending with the traditional school year—September through June. The last section contains activities for some patriotic and national holidays. These celebrations occur throughout the year, including the summer months.

For every holiday in this book, there are teacher lesson pages and accompanying student activity pages. The teacher lesson pages provide the following information.

- *Background*—The information tells when each holiday is observed and gives a short history.
- *Setting Up the Center*—The set up includes the holiday sign and the types of pictures to display, suggestions for the Surprise Box, titles of books or magazines related to the holiday or relevant topics, and some technology resources.
- *Center Activities*—This section describes activities that students can complete independently or in cooperative learning groups. All activities include the objectives, curriculum connections, materials, and directions.

## Suggested Books

This reading list provides suggestions for high-quality children's literature selections that pertain to the holiday or related topics. Some are easy to read, allowing students to enjoy them independently. Others are more difficult and can be read aloud to the class or read by cooperative learning groups. Both readers and non-readers will enjoy the beautiful illustrations that appear in many of the books.

## Technology Resources

The resource list for technology can include software (disk and/or CD-ROM), videotapes, laserdiscs, and cassette tapes. Utilization of technology will depend on the type of equipment that is available to you and your students.

## Center Activities

Every activity in this book can be correlated with one or more of the major curriculum areas. As a result, students will benefit from the time they spend using these activities. A lesson plan that includes a clearly stated objective, the curriculum connection, a list of materials needed, and describes any necessary teacher preparation is provided for each activity. Directions on the activity pages help make the projects easy and fun for students to complete.

Retain the activities in the center for at least one week per holiday. In most cases, the center can be changed from one holiday to the next. If there is a substantial block of time before the next holiday, you may wish to organize your center in one of the following ways:

1. *Patriotic/National Holidays:* Study some patriotic/national holidays during one week. They are grouped together in this book for easy reference.
2. *Seasonal:* Create a few activities to investigate the uniqueness of each season.
3. *Birthdays:* Make some activities to celebrate all of the children's birthdays at once and to learn about the significance of birthdays.

# Holiday Calendar

| SEPTEMBER |
| --- |
| Week 1 Labor Day |
| Week 2 |
| Week 3 |
| Week 4 |

| OCTOBER |
| --- |
| Week 1 |
| Week 2 Columbus Day |
| Week 3 |
| Week 4 Halloween |

| NOVEMBER |
| --- |
| Week 1 Election Day |
| Week 2 Veterans Day |
| Week 3 Thanksgiving |
| Week 4 |

| DECEMBER |
| --- |
| Week 1 Hanukkah |
| Week 2 |
| Week 3 Christmas |
| Week 4 Kwanzaa |

| JANUARY |
| --- |
| Week 1 New Year's |
| Week 2 Martin Luther King Jr. Day |
| Week 3 |
| Week 4 |

| FEBRUARY |
| --- |
| Week 1 |
| Week 2 Valentine's Day |
| Week 3 Presidents' Day |
| Week 4 |

| MARCH |
| --- |
| Week 1 |
| Week 2 |
| Week 3 St. Patrick's Day |
| Week 4 |

| APRIL |
| --- |
| Week 1 Easter (varies) |
| Week 2 |
| Week 3 Earth Day |
| Week 4 |

| MAY |
| --- |
| Week 1 Cinco de Mayo |
| Week 2 Mother's Day |
| Week 3 |
| Week 4 Memorial Day |

| JUNE |
| --- |
| Week 1 |
| Week 2 Flag Day, Father's Day |
| Week 3 |
| Week 4 |

| JULY |
| --- |
| Week 1 Canada Day, Independence Day |
| Week 2 Bastille Day |
| Week 3 |
| Week 4 |

| AUGUST |
| --- |
| Week 1 |
| Week 2 |
| Week 3 |
| Week 4 |

# Center Rules

1. Use quiet voices.

2. Clean up.

3. Cooperate with others.

4. Have fun!

# Holiday Center Sign

# Holiday Clip Art

Hanukkah

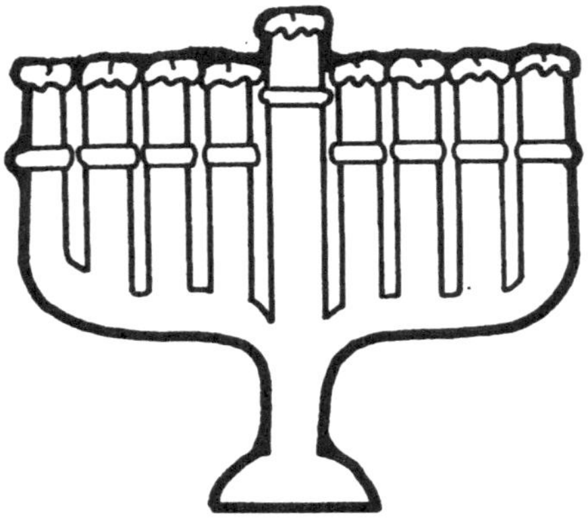

Halloween

Christmas

Christmas

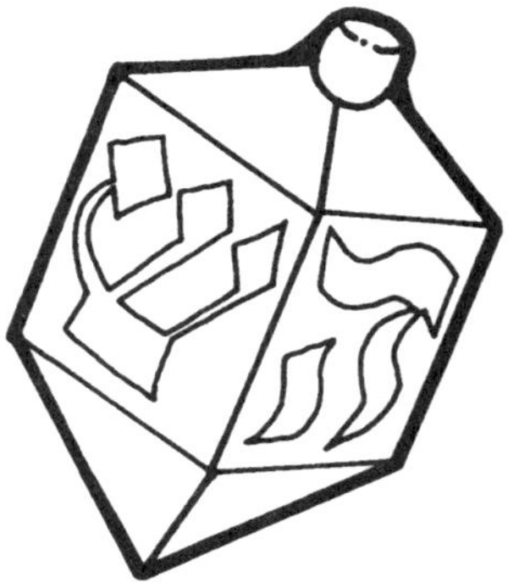

Hanukkah

Flag of Mexico

Thanksgiving

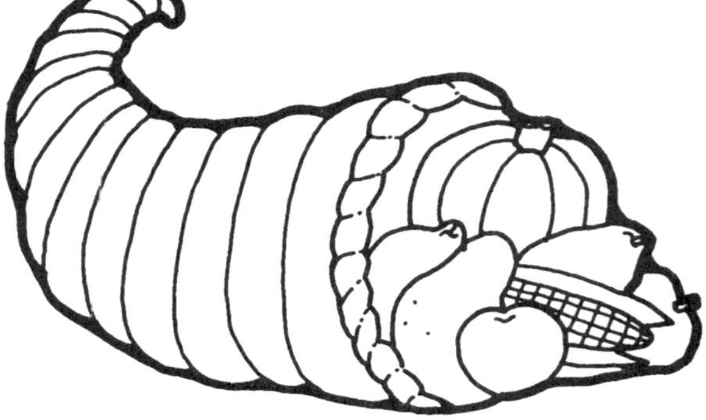

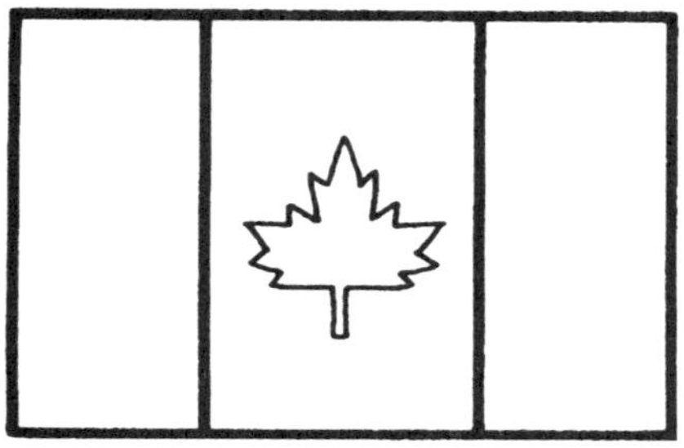

Flag of Canada

 

# Holiday Clip Art *(cont.)*

Presidents' Day

St. Patrick's Day

Kwanzaa

Martin Luther King, Jr. Day

Labor Day

# Holiday Clip Art *(cont.)*

Easter

Mother's Day

Father's Day

Earth Day

Valentine's Day

Patriotic Holidays

 

# Labor Day

## Background

In the United States, the first Monday in September is set aside to honor workers. The first Labor Day was celebrated in 1882. It became a legal holiday in 1894. It was originally organized to recognize factory workers and the need for labor reform. Labor Day activities often include parades, picnics, and family get-togethers. Traditionally, this holiday signals the end of summer and the beginning of the new school year. Many other countries also have Labor Day celebrations, some of which are held on May Day (May 1).

## Setting Up the Center

Prepare a *Labor Day* sign. Color, laminate, and post it in the center. To decorate the center, have students cut and paste magazine pictures that show people at work.

- ***Surprise Box***

a clip-on name badge, a time card, an engraved nameplate, items that are used in specific jobs such as chalk for a teacher or a toy wrench for a carpenter

- ***Suggested Books***

  Display books about various occupations.
  *Daddies at Work* by Eve Merriam (S&S Trade, 1989)
  *Mommies at Work* by Eve Merriam (S&S Trade, 1989)
  *Things People Do* by Anne Civardi (EDC, 1986)

## Center Activities

- ***"What I Want to Do" Collage***

**Objectives:** To picture themselves in 20 years; to examine various career options; to consider what they enjoy doing

**Curriculum Connection:** social studies

**Materials:** old magazines; scissors; glue sticks; 8" x 10" (20 cm x 26 cm) white poster board, one per student; colored markers or crayons

**Directions:** Students make collages using magazine pictures that represent the occupations and hobbies they might like to do in the future.

- ***Job Hats Matching Activity***

**Objectives:** To understand that there are many different jobs in each community; to match various uniforms with their corresponding hats

**Curriculum Connection:** social studies

**Materials:** Job Hats (pages 14-15), scissors, skin-tone colored construction paper, markers

**Preparation:** Reproduce pages 14-15 on construction paper. Cut out the figures and hats. Color the hats and uniforms. Number each hat and corresponding uniform on the back for self-checking purposes. Laminate and cut out the pieces. Cut a slit in each hat so it will fit any figure's head. Place the pieces in a resealable plastic bag. Put the bag in a Job Hats folder. Write or cut and glue, the directions on the folder.

**Directions:** Students place the hats on the figures by matching them to the corresponding uniforms. Self-checking is done by comparing the numbers on the backs of the figures and hats.

# Job Hats

**Directions:** Match the hats with the uniforms these people are wearing. Put a hat on each person. Check yourself by looking at the numbers on the backs of the pieces.

# Job Hats *(cont.)*

**Directions:** Match the hats with the uniforms the figures are wearing. Put a hat on each figure. Check yourself by looking at the numbers on the backs of the pieces.

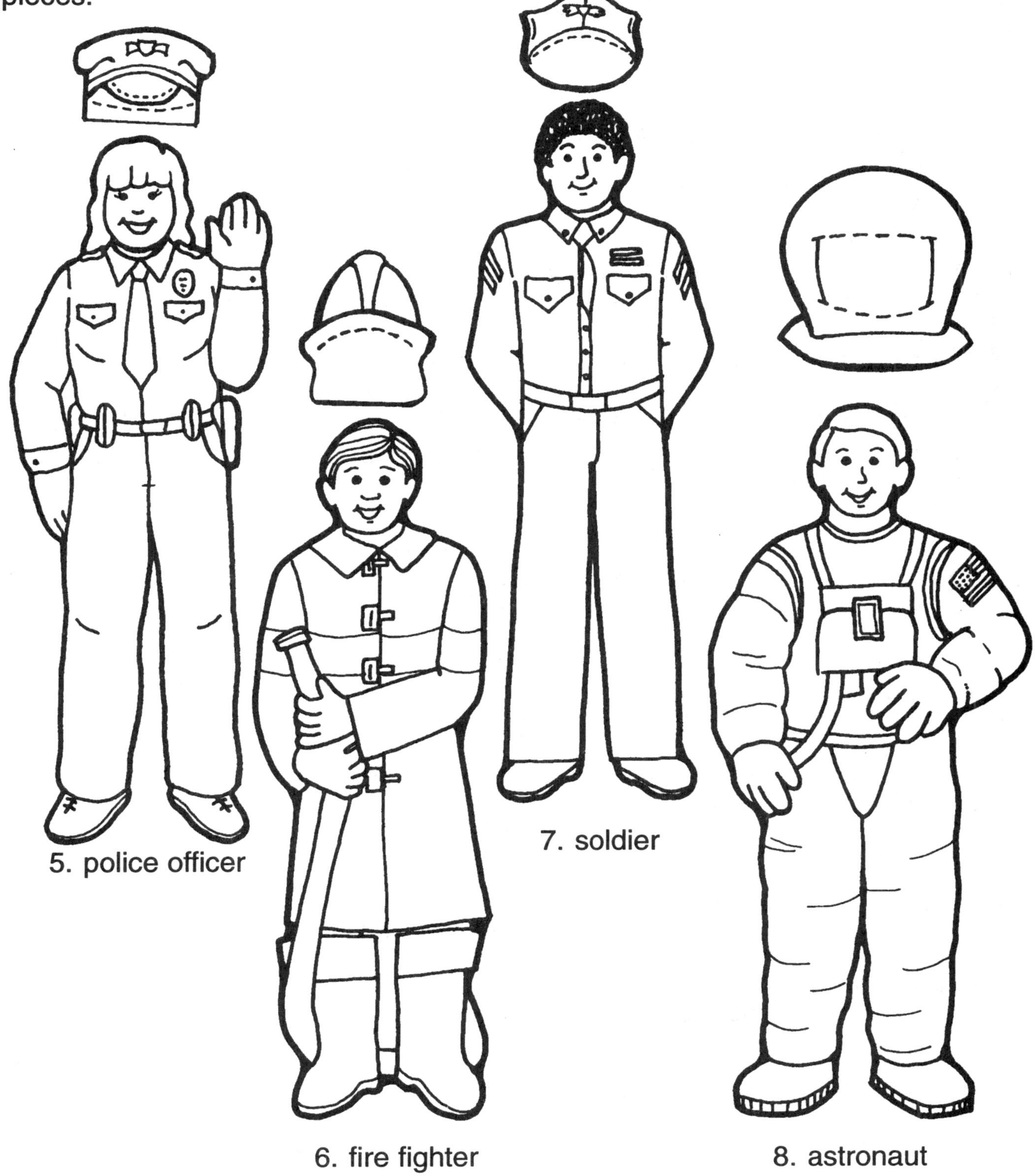

# Halloween

## Background

Children love this holiday that both frightens and delights. October 31 was originally set aside as a Celtic celebration of the dead. However, today Halloween is commonly known as a time for children to wear costumes and go trick-or-treating for candy and other goodies. Black, because it symbolizes death, and orange are the traditional colors. Symbols for this occasion include pumpkins, jack-o'-lanterns, ghosts, black cats, bats, and witches.

## Setting Up the Center

Use the clip art (page 10) to prepare a *Halloween* sign. Color, laminate, and post it in the center. To decorate the center, create a spider to put on a string web, hang a ghost made from an old white sheet, use real pumpkins and/or have students make papier maché pumpkins and jack-o'-lanterns.

- ***Surprise Box***

small plastic spider, miniature pumpkin, candy wrapper

- ***Suggested Books***

*Arthur's Halloween* by Marc Brown (Little, Brown & Co., 1983)
*The Biggest Pumpkin Ever* by Steven Kroll (Holiday House, 1984)
*Halloween Cats* by Jean Marzollo (Scholastic, 1992)
*Halloween Mask for Monster* by Virginia Mueller (Viking, 1986)
*Halloween Parade* by Harriet Ziefert (Viking, 1992)
*Humbug Witch* by Lorna Balian (Abingdon, 1965)
*My First Halloween* by Tomie dePaola (Putnam, 1991)
*Pumpkin Light* by David Ray (Putnam, 1993)
*Pumpkin Pumpkin* by Jeanne Titherington (Scholastic, 1986)

- ***Technology Resources***

*Cranberry Halloween.* (Filmstrip and cassette; video); 11 min. Pied Piper/AIMS Multimedia, 9710 De Soto Ave., Chatsworth, CA 91311; 1-800-367-2567.

*The Dancing Skeleton.* (Video); 10 min. SRA, P.O. Box 543, Blacklick, OH 43004; 1-800-843-8855.

*Halloween Party.* (Video); 8 min. Troll Associates, Catalog Sales Dept., 100 Corporate Dr., Mahwah, NJ 07498; 1-800-929-8765.

*Halloween Surprises.* (Videotape/Videodisc by Disney Educational Products); 13 min. Available from Coronet/MTI Film and Video, P.O. Box 2649, Columbus, OH 43216; 1-800-321-3106.

*Joey and the Jack-O'-Lantern.* (Video); 7 min. Troll Associates, Catalog Sales Dept., 100 Corporate Dr., Mahwah, NJ 07498; 1-800-929-8765.

*A Spooky Tale for Halloween.* (Video); 5 min. Troll Associates, Catalog Sales Dept., 100 Corporate Dr., Mahwah, NJ 07498; 1-800-929-8765.

*That Terrible Halloween Night.* (Video); 8 min. SRA, P.O. Box 543, Blacklick, OH 43004; 1-800-843-8855.

# Halloween *(cont.)*

## Center Activities

- ***Masquerade Mask***

**Objective:** To encourage creativity

**Curriculum Connection:** art

**Materials:** tagboard Masquerade Mask pattern (page 18), one per student; craft sticks, one per student; resealable plastic bags with decorating supplies: sequins, rick-rack, yarn, feathers, plastic coins, pipe cleaners, stickers, etc.

**Preparation:** Trace a mask pattern on tagboard for each student. Place the tagboard patterns in a Halloween Mask folder. In resealable plastic bags, organize the various decorating supplies. Put all the plastic bags into one supply basket.

**Directions:** Students cut out the mask shapes and create their own spectacular designs. When the masks are complete, they can glue craft sticks to one side for holding the masks.

- ***Halloween Word Games***

**Objective:** To practice critical thinking skills

**Curriculum Connection:** language arts

**Materials:** Halloween Word Games (page 19), scratch paper, pencils

**Preparation:** Cut off the answer key at the bottom of page 19. Make one copy of the page, tape it inside a Halloween Word Games folder, laminate the folder, and post it in the center.

**Directions:** Students will use scratch paper to figure out the coded message and unscramble the candy names.

- ***Scratch Drawing***

**Objective:** To encourage creativity

**Curriculum Connection:** art

**Materials:** white paper, orange and black crayons, pencils

**Preparation:** Separate a few orange and black crayons into a resealable plastic bag. Set a stack of white paper, along with the bag of crayons, in a basket. Make a sample of the project for students to see and post it in the center.

**Directions:** Students will heavily color a large section of the paper with orange crayon and then completely and heavily cover the paper with black crayon. They will use their pencils to scratch Halloween designs on the paper. The black will scratch off allowing the orange to show.

- ***Pattern Faces***

**Objective:** To explore shape combinations

**Curriculum Connection:** math

**Materials:** pattern blocks, Pumpkin Pattern (page 20)

**Preparation:** Reproduce the Pumpkin Pattern on heavy orange paper and laminate.

**Directions:** Students will use pattern blocks to make original jack-o'-lantern faces on the Pumpkin Pattern.

**Option:** Reproduce the Pumpkin Pattern, and have students draw and color their favorite shapes to create jack-o'-lantern faces.

# Masquerade Mask

**Directions:** Cut out and decorate your mask. When you are finished, glue a craft stick on to one side. Allow the glue to dry. Then try on your mask, holding it by the craft stick.

# Halloween Word Games

## Halloween Message

**Code**

| A | C | D | E | F | G | H | I | L |
|---|---|---|---|---|---|---|---|---|
| ▼ | ❉ | ❥ | ✙ | ● | ◆ | ❒ | ◗ | ✔ |
| **N** | **O** | **P** | **R** | **S** | **T** | **U** | **W** | **Y** |
| ✪ | ✚ | ✽ | ✜ | = | ❖ | ❀ | ➽ | ✹ |

___ ___________ ___ ___ ______, ___ _

●✚✜ ❒▼✔✔✚➽✙✙✪ ●❀✪ ▼✪❥ =▼●✙❖✹ ❀=✙ ▼

__________, __ ____ __ _____, ___

●✔▼=❒✔◗◆❒❖ ◆✚ ➽◗❖❒ ▼✪ ▼❥❀✔❖ ▼✪❥

___ ____ _______ _____.

✙▼❖ ✚✪✔✹ ➽✜▼✽✽✙❥ ❉▼✪❥✹

## Candy Scrambles

naycd rab ____________________

lubbbe umg ____________________

rahd acdny ____________________

accehltoo ____________________

ifutr eshwc ____________________

acmarle ____________________

---

## Answer Key

**Halloween Message:**

For Halloween fun and safety, use a flashlight, go with an adult, and eat only wrapped candy.

**Candy Scrambles:**

candy bar, bubble gum, hard candy, chocolate, fruit chews, caramel

# Pumpkin Pattern

**Directions:** Make a jack-o'-lantern face using pattern block shapes.

# Thanksgiving

## Background

Many cultures, religions, and countries around the world celebrate some kind of holiday that involves giving thanks. In the United States, Thanksgiving is celebrated on the fourth Thursday in November. This harvest celebration of Thanksgiving dates back to 1621 when the Pilgrims had settled the Plymouth Colony. They had managed to live through a difficult winter with the help of the Native Americans who lived in the area. The Pilgrims invited their new friends to a feast during which they gave thanks for their survival and their harvest. Surprisingly, Thanksgiving did not become an annual event throughout America until 1864. Today people continue to enjoy eating Thanksgiving feasts and spending time with their families. Symbols for this occasion include turkeys, cornucopias full of harvest bounty, fall leaves, Pilgrims, and Native Americans.

## Setting Up the Center

Use the clip art (page 10) to prepare a *Thanksgiving* sign. Color, laminate, and post it in the center. Decorate the center with a cornucopia full of plastic, wax, or papier mâché harvest foods.

- ***Surprise Box***

a miniature ear of Indian corn, a toy turkey, a sugar cone (to symbolize a cornucopia), a feather

- ***Suggested Books***

  *Arthur's Thanksgiving* by Marc Brown (Little, Brown & Company, 1983)

  *Best Thanksgiving Book* by Pat Whitehead (Troll, 1985)

  *The First Thanksgiving* by Linda Hayward (Random House, 1990)

  *Mousekin's Thanksgiving* by Edna Miller (Simon and Schuster, 1985)

  *Oh, What a Thanksgiving* by Steven Kroll (Scholastic, 1988)

  *The Pilgrim's First Thanksgiving* by Ann McGovern (Scholastic, 1993)

  *Samuel Eaton's Day* by Kate Waters (Scholastic, 1993)

  *Sarah Morton's Day* by Kate Waters (Scholastic, 1989)

  *Silly Tilly's Thanksgiving Dinner* by Lillian Hoban (Harper Trophy, 1990)

  *Thanksgiving at Our House* by Wendy Watson (Clarion, 1991)

  *Turkey for Thanksgiving* by Eve Bunting (Houghton Mifflin, 1991)

  *Turkey's Gift to the People* by Ani Rucki (Scholastic, 1992)

  *Turkey's Side of It: Adam Joshua's Thanksgiving* by Janice Lee Smith (HarperCollins, 1990)

- ***Technology Resources***

*Cranberry Thanksgiving.* (Filmstrip and cassette; video); 11 min. Pied Piper/AIMS Multimedia, 9710 De Soto Ave., Chatsworth, CA 91311; 1-800-367-2567.

*The First Thanksgiving.* (Video); 7 min. Troll Associates, Catalog Sales Dept. 100 Corporate Dr., Mahwah, NJ, 07498; 1-800-929-8765.

*How Many Days to America? A Thanksgiving Story.* (Video); 11 min. Coronet/MTI Film and Video, P.O. Box 2649, Columbus, OH 43216; 1-800-321-3106.

# Thanksgiving *(cont.)*

## Center Activities

- ***Let's Talk Turkey***

**Objective:** To practice math facts

**Curriculum Connection:** math

**Materials:** brown construction paper; scraps of red, orange, yellow, and tan construction paper; glue; markers

**Preparation:** Trace and cut out a handprint from brown paper. Make one additional cutout of each finger from the scraps (red, orange, yellow, tan). Glue the colored finger cutouts onto the brown fingers of the handprint, leaving the top inch (2.5 cm) unglued. Draw a turkey face on the thumb, and write a math equation on each colored fingertip. The corresponding answers go underneath on the brown fingertips. You can increase the number of math facts students practice by using both sides of each handprint turkey or by making multiple handprint turkeys.

**Directions:** Students solve the math equations, then check themselves by looking at the answers underneath the colored fingertips.

- ***Food Sorting***

**Objective:** To practice sorting food cards into groups

**Curriculum Connections:** science, health

**Materials:** 2 copies of Cornucopia Pattern (page 23), Cornucopia Food Cards (pages 24-25), construction paper (white and brown; other colors, optional), scissors

**Preparation:** Reproduce the Cornucopia Food Cards. Glue them onto white or colored construction paper. Then cut out the cards and laminate them. Copy the two cornucopia patterns on to brown construction paper. Cut out the patterns and staple them together, leaving the mouth open as a pocket. Place the food cards in the cornucopia, put the activity in a Food Sorting folder, and write or glue the directions on the outside of the folder.

**Directions:** Students remove the food cards from the cornucopia and sort them into piles of healthful foods and extra foods. They could also sort by most liked and least liked, by meals (breakfast, lunch, and dinner), or foods that were eaten by the Pilgrims and foods that were not eaten by the Pilgrims.

- ***Native American Pictographs***

**Objective:** To use reasoning skills to interpret traditional Native American picture symbols

**Curriculum Connections:** language arts, social studies

**Materials:** Native American Pictographs (page 26), brown paper bag, construction paper

**Preparation:** Reproduce the pictograph cards on construction paper. Laminate them, and cut them out. Cut a few blank cards from construction paper for students to make their own pictographs, relating to the lives of Native Americans or their own lives. Tear paper bag panels and wrinkle them. Then straighten them out to look like leather. Tell students to pretend these are pieces of leather. Ask them to write their pictograph messages on the "leather."

**Directions:** Students can use the pictograph cards to make up their own messages for other students to decipher.

 

# Cornucopia Pattern

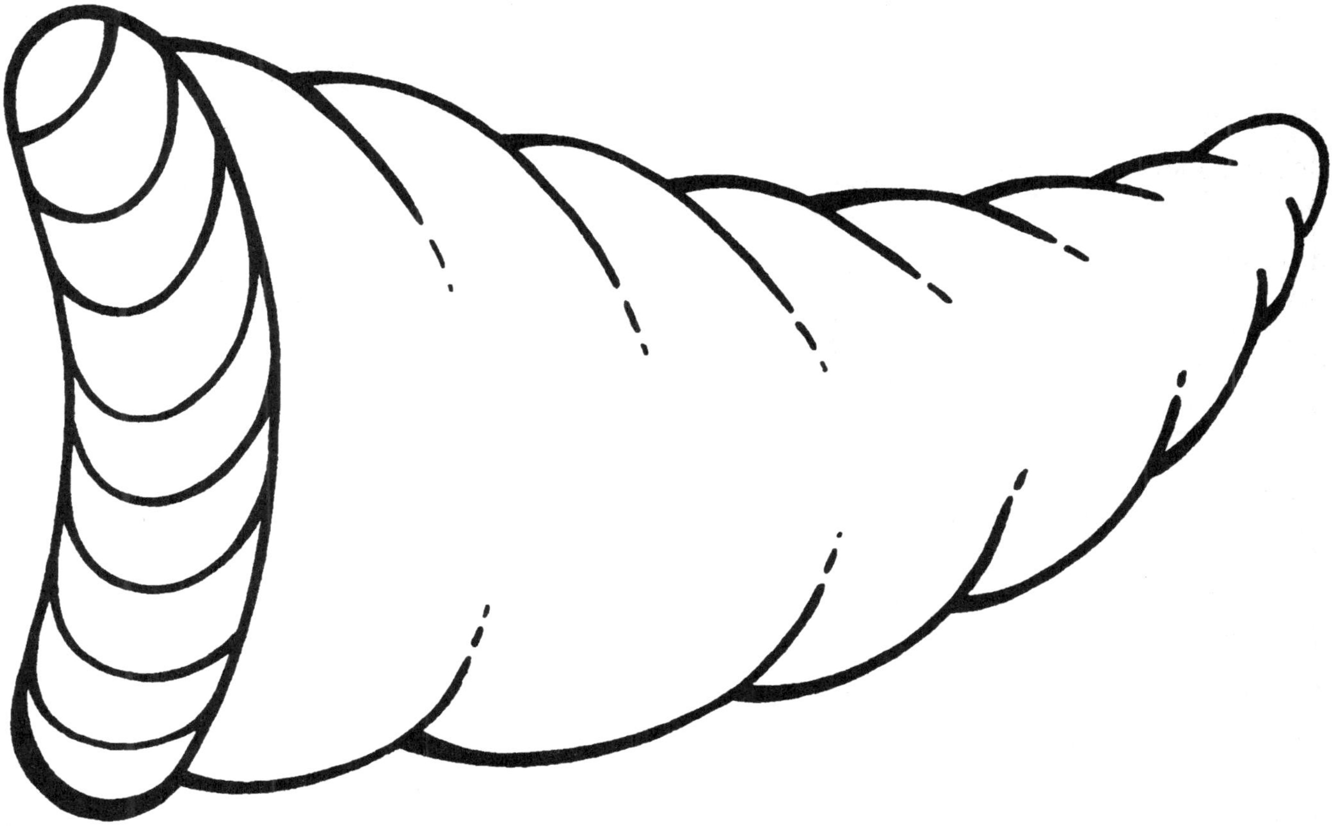

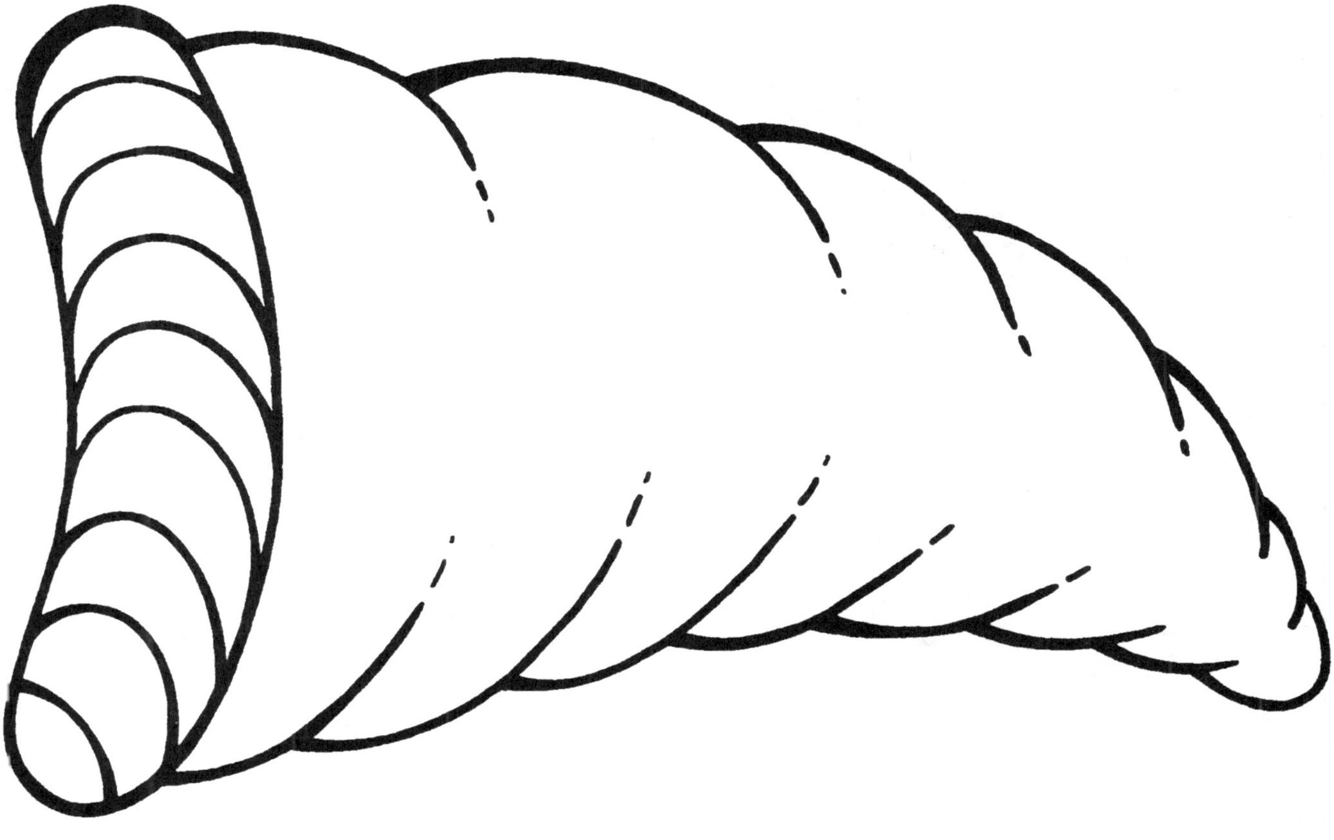

# Cornucopia Food Cards

banana

apple

strawberry

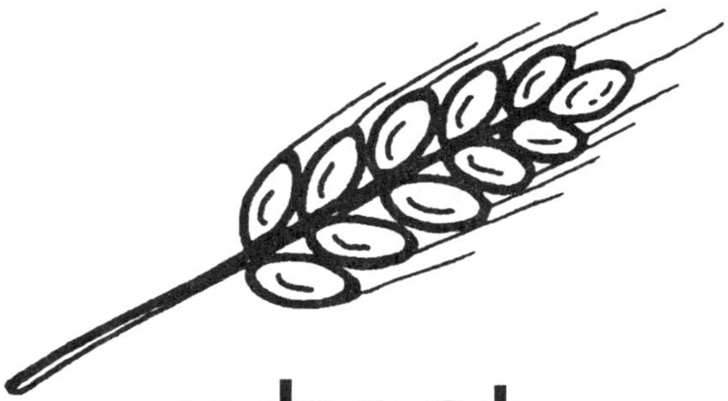

wheat

corn

rice

chicken

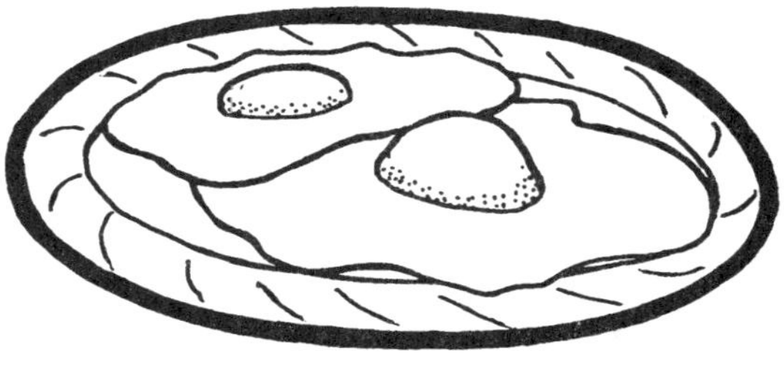

eggs

 

# Cornucopia Food Cards *(cont.)*

cake

candy bar

oatmeal

pumpkin

soda

broccoli

carrots

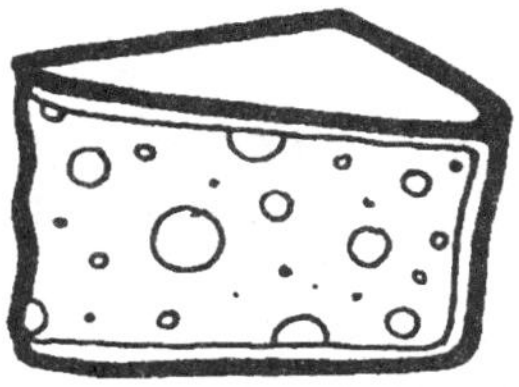

cheese

# Native American Pictographs

**Directions:** Use the pictographs to write a message to a friend.

| | | | |
|---|---|---|---|
| man |  | mountain |  |
| woman |  | river |  |
| teepee |  | forest |  |
| sun | 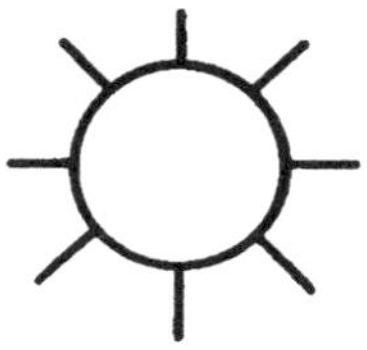 | plains |  |
| horse |  | hunt | 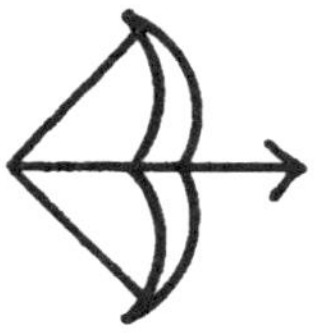 |
| deer |  | catch |  |
| fish |  | go | 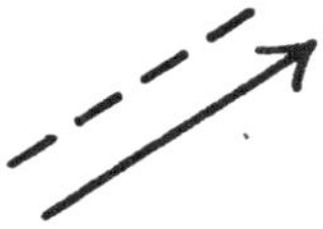 |
| (bison commonly known as) buffalo |  | meet |  |

 

# Hanukkah

## Background

The Jewish holiday of Hanukkah (or Chanukah) is also called the Festival of Lights. It is usually celebrated during December although in some years it may start in November. It commemorates the victory of the Maccabees over the large army of the Syrian king, Antiochus IV, in 165 B.C., as well as the universal message that all people have the right to be free.

After the Jews had won their battle, they went to their temple and found that the Syrians had brought in statues of their own gods. The eternal light had been allowed to go out. The Jews rekindled the light, but they had only enough oil to keep it burning for one day, and it would take a messenger eight days to get more oil. The miracle of Hanukkah is that the oil kept burning for eight days. This was long enough for the messenger to return with more oil. Jews use a candleholder called a *menorah* to symbolize this miracle. It holds nine candles. The center candle, the *shamus,* is used to light the other eight.

Today, the eight-day holiday is celebrated by lighting the candles of the menorah, playing games of chance with a spinning top called a *dreidel,* and eating special holiday foods such as potato pancakes called *latkes.* Children often receive a gift on each night of Hanukkah in addition to Hanukkah *gelt* (money). This gelt sometimes consists of chocolate wrapped in gold foil to look like money.

## Setting Up the Center

Use the clip art (page 10) to prepare a *Hanukkah* sign. Color, laminate, and post it in the center. You may wish to decorate the center with small wrapped empty packages or small bags of play money coins.

- ***Surprise Box***

candle, potato, gelt (or chocolate coins), wooden or plastic dreidel

- ***Suggested Books***

*All the Lights in the Night* by Arthur A. Levine (Tambourine Books, 1991)

*Hanukkah* by Miriam Nerlove (Albert Whitman, 1992)

*Hanukkah!* by Roni Schotter (Little, Brown & Co., 1993)

*Hanukkah Lights, Hanukkah Nights* by Leslie Kimmelman (Harper Row, 1992)

*Hanukkah, Oh Hanukkah!: A Treasury of Stories, Songs, and Games to Share* by Wendy Wax (Bantam, 1993)

*Happy Hanukkah Rebus* by David A. Adler (Viking, 1989)

*Latkes and Applesauce* by Fran Manushkin (Scholastic, 1990)

*The Story of Hanukkah* by Amy Erlich (Dial, 1989)

- ***Technology Resource***

*Hanukkah.* (Video); 10 min. Pied Piper/AIMS Multimedia, 9710 De Soto Ave., Chatsworth, CA 91311; 1-800-367-2567.

# Hanukkah *(cont.)*

## Center Activities

- ***3-D Dreidel***

**Objectives:** To create an ornamental dreidel; To promote cultural awareness

**Curriculum Connection:** art

**Materials:** Dreidel Pattern (page 29), one copy per student; scissors; hole punch; 12" (30 cm) piece of ribbon, string, or yarn per student

**Preparation:** Reproduce the Dreidel Pattern on white or yellow heavy paper. Place the copies and pieces of ribbon, string, or yarn into a 3-D Dreidel folder. Prepare a sample to display.

**Directions:** Each student will cut out both dreidel patterns. They will cut a slit from the top to the middle of one pattern and from the bottom to the middle of the other pattern. Students will form 3-D dreidels by sliding the two patterns together at the slits. They will punch a hole in the top and thread a piece of ribbon, string, or yarn through the hole.

**Option:** Before sliding the pattern pieces together at the slits, students can copy the four Hebrew letters (page 30) on their dreidels.

- ***The Dreidel Game***

**Objectives:** To learn how to play a children's game from another culture; to promote cultural awareness

**Curriculum Connection:** social studies

**Materials:** a wooden dreidel or copies of The Dreidel Game (page 30), one per student; short sharpened pencils, one per student; scissors; glue or tape

**Preparation:** Reproduce The Dreidel Game on white paper. Put the copies and a plastic bag of pencils in The Dreidel Game folder. Make a sample dreidel to display in the center.

**Directions:** Students cut along the solid lines of the dreidel and fold along the dotted lines to make a box. They can tape or glue the tabs. They carefully poke a pencil through the holes to make the spinner of the dreidel. Instructions for playing the game are given on page 30.

- ***Making Latkes***

**Objective:** To promote cultural awareness; to practice sequencing a list of details using a recipe from another culture

**Curriculum Connections:** language arts, social studies

**Materials:** construction paper, two copies of Making Latkes (page 31), scissors

**Preparation:** Reproduce the sentence strips for Making Latkes on construction paper. Tape one copy to the inside of a Potato Pancakes folder as an answer key. Laminate the other copy, and cut apart the strips. Shuffle the strips to rearrange the order. Then place them in a resealable plastic bag. Write or glue the directions on the outside of the folder.

**Directions:** Students will put the sentence strips in order to correctly sequence a recipe for potato pancakes.

**Options:** Have students follow the recipe to make latkes. Allow them to taste the latkes. You may also wish to have students use a recipe to make applesauce to enjoy with the latkes. Be sure to ask parents if their children have any food allergies or dietary restrictions.

# Dreidel Pattern

**Directions:** Cut out and color the two pieces of the dreidel. Cut along each dashed line. Slip the pieces together as shown. Tape them in the creases. Punch a hole in the top. Thread a piece of yarn, string, or ribbon through the hole.

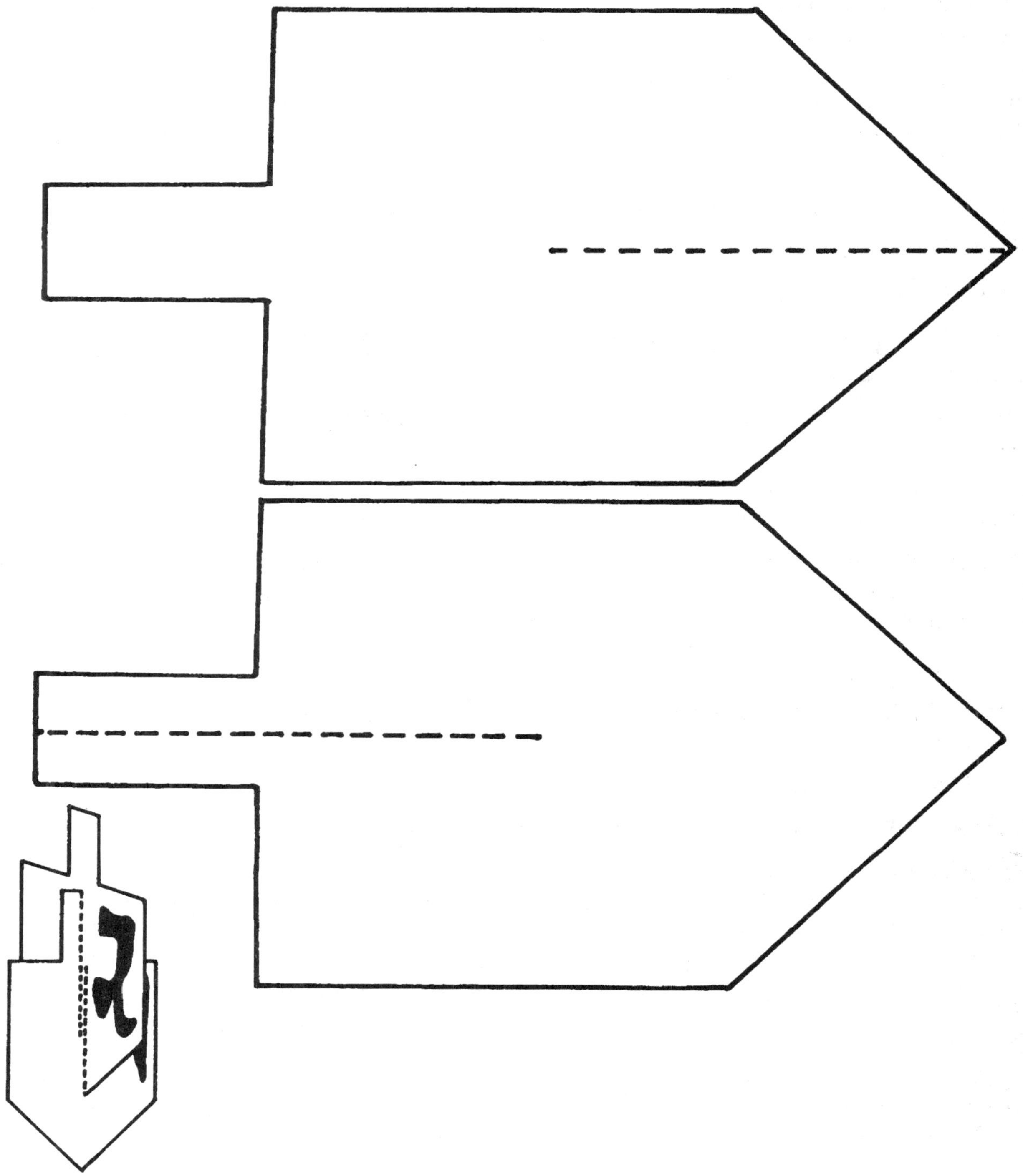

# The Dreidel Game

**Directions for making a dreidel:** Cut out the dreidel along the solid lines. Make two small holes where the circles are on the top and bottom. Fold it along the dotted lines, and glue or tape it together so you have a box shape. Push a short pencil through. Spin the dreidel by twirling the pencil.

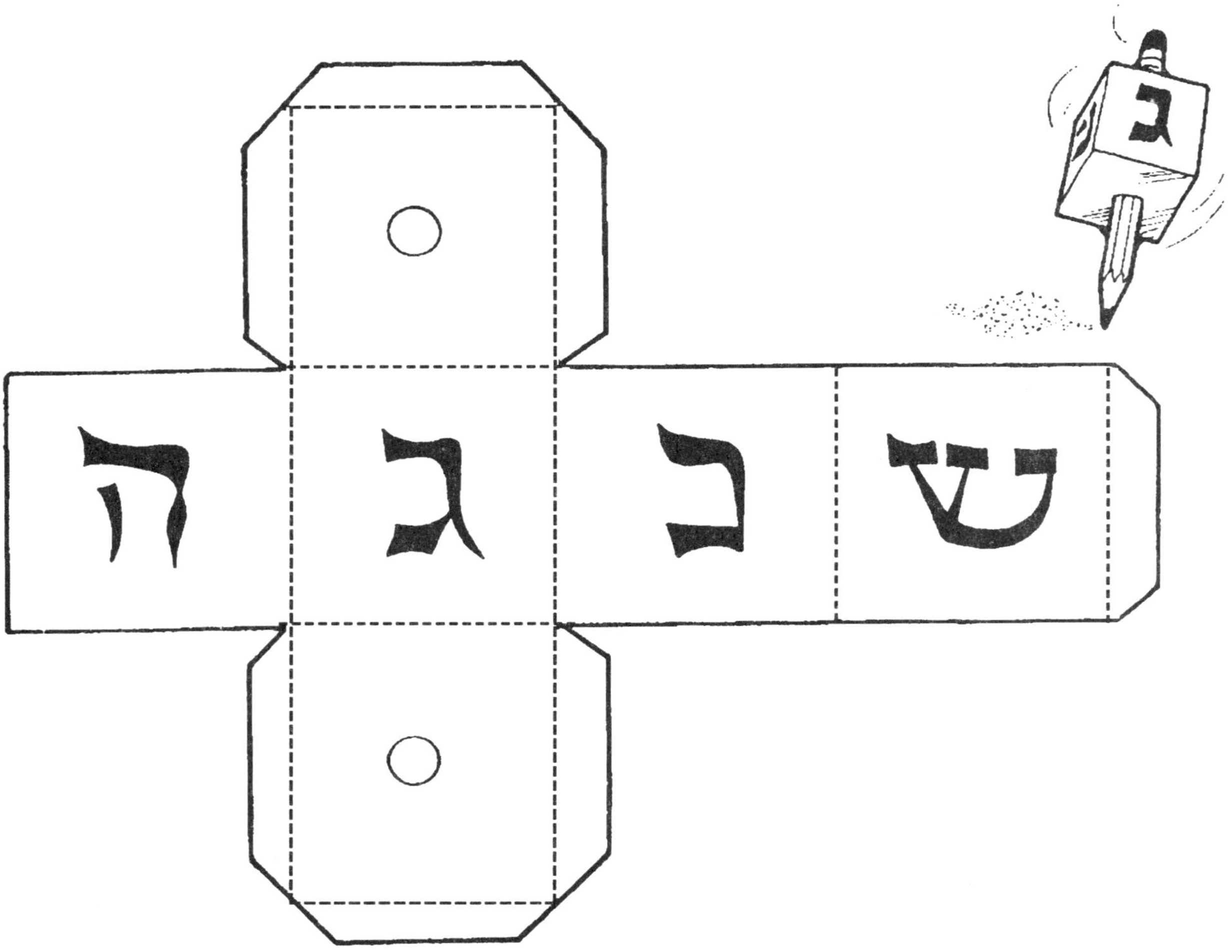


**Directions for Playing the Dreidel Game:** The dreidel is a four-sided top. Each side has a Hebrew letter on it: *nun* ( נ ), *gimmel* ( ג ), *hay* ( ה ), and *shin* ( ש ). These four letters stand for the Hebrew words that mean "a great miracle happened here." The players sit in a circle. Each player receives an equal number of tokens (buttons, nuts, gelt) and puts five from his or her pile into the center. Everyone takes turns spinning the dreidel. The letter on top when the dreidel stops spinning tells you what to do. *Nun:* Do nothing. *Gimmel:* Take the center pile. *Hay:* Take half the center pile. *Shin:* Give half of your pile. Players who lose all of their tokens are out of the game. The last player with tokens is the winner.

 

# Making Latkes

**Directions:** Put the sentence strips in the correct order.

Wash three potatoes.

Peel and grate the potatoes.

Drain the grated potatoes in a colander.

Mix in 2 teaspoons (10 mL) of grated onion, 1 egg, and 6 tablespoons (90 mL) of flour.

After mixing all of the ingredients, carefully heat 4 tablespoons (60 mL) of oil in a skillet.

Drop one tablespoon (15 mL) of the potato mixture at a time into the oil.

Use a spatula to turn the latke over so that it browns on both sides.

Place the latkes on a plate.

Serve the latkes with applesauce or sour cream.

# Christmas

## Background

Christmas, the celebration of the birth of Christ, is one of the most popular holidays all over the world. Many families attend church, exchange presents, and enjoy a feast. Santa Claus, whose name varies from country to country, is said to spend Christmas Eve (December 24th) guiding his reindeer powered sleigh all over the world to deliver gifts. A traditional Christmas includes decorated trees, Christmas lights, wreaths hung on doors, stockings filled with goodies, nativity scenes, presents, singing Christmas carols, and plates of baked goods. In this celebration of joy to the world, people focus their thoughts on peace, kindness, family, and sharing with those in need.

## Setting Up the Center

Use the clip art (page 10) to prepare a *Christmas* sign. Color, laminate, and post it in the center. You may wish to provide some tapes of Christmas music for students to enjoy.

- ***Surprise Box***

package bow, small clump of pine tree needles, plastic star, Christmas tree cookie cutter

- ***Suggested Books***

  *The Christmas Star* by Marcus Pfister (North-South Books, 1993)
  *An Early American Christmas* by Tomie dePaola (Holiday House, 1987)
  *How the Grinch Stole Christmas* by Dr. Seuss (Random House, 1957)
  *I Spy Christmas Photos* by Walter Wick, riddles by Jean Marzollo (Scholastic, 1992)
  *The Jolly Christmas Postman* by Janet & Allan Ahlberg (Little Brown & Co., 1991)
  *The Night Before Christmas* by Clement C. Moore (Knopf, 1984)
  *The Twelve Days of Christmas* by Jan Geddes (Ledco, 1995)
  *The Wild Christmas Reindeer* by Jan Brett (G.P. Putnam's Sons, 1990)

- ***Technology Resources***

*Cranberry Christmas.* (Filmstrip and cassette; video); 11 min. Pied Piper/AIMS Multimedia, 9710 De Soto Ave., Chatsworth, CA 91311; 1-800-367-2567.

*Holiday Facts and Fun: A Multicultural Christmas.* (Video); 17 min. Pied Piper/AIMS Multimedia, 9710 De Soto Ave., Chatsworth, CA 91311; 1-800-367-2567.

*The Night Before Christmas.* (Video); 10 min. Pied Piper/AIMS Multimedia, 9710 De Soto Ave., Chatsworth, CA 91311; 1-800-367-2567.

## Center Activities

- ***Lift the Gift***

**Objective:** To practice matching antonyms

**Curriculum Connection:** language arts

**Materials:** Lift the Gift (pages 34-35), tagboard, glue, craft knife

**Preparation:** Glue the Lift the Gift pages onto tagboard. Use a craft knife to cut along the dotted lines of each gift. Carefully glue the gift page on top of the page with no gifts, so that the words show when the flaps are raised. Be sure you do not glue down the flaps. Place the activity in a Lift the Gift folder.

**Directions:** Students will test their knowledge of antonyms by determining the opposite of the word on each package. They check their answers by lifting the flap on the side of each gift.

# Christmas *(cont.)*

## Center Activities *(cont.)*

- ***Christmas Wrap Around the World***

**Objectives:** To examine linguistic differences; to distinguish the different ways people say "Merry Christmas"

**Curriculum Connection:** social studies

**Materials:** Christmas Wrap Around the World (page 36), tagboard, 12" (30 cm) piece of red or green yarn, hole punch or thread

**Preparation:** Glue the Christmas Wrap Around the World onto tagboard. Cut out the front and back match them and glue the pieces of tagboard together. Laminate. Tie up one end of the yarn to the card. Place in a Christmas Wrap Around the World folder.

**Directions:** Students match the name of the language with the correct way to say Merry Christmas by wrapping the yarn around the card from left to right making sure to secure the yarn in the notches. The answers on the back of the card can be used for self-checking.

- ***Christmas Poet-Tree***

**Objective:** To create an original poem

**Curriculum Connection:** language arts

**Materials:** Christmas Poet-Tree Pattern (page 37), green construction paper, white tagboard, Christmas Poet-Tree Word Cards (page 38), Velcro, scissors

**Preparation:** Reproduce the tree pattern on green construction paper and laminate it. Reproduce the word cards on tagboard, laminate them, and cut them out. Attach a piece of Velcro® to the back of each word card and on the tree. Place in a Christmas Poet-Tree folder.

**Directions:** Students can arrange words in any order to make poems about Christmas trees.

- ***Christmas Gift List***

**Objectives:** To encourage students to think about the spirit of giving; To practice making lists

**Curriculum Connection:** language arts

**Materials:** Christmas Gift List (page 39), one per student

**Preparation:** Reproduce the pattern on white paper and place in a Christmas List folder.

**Directions:** Students will write things that they can give and receive at Christmas that do not cost any money. Encourage them to write different ideas for each list.

- ***Christmas Card Rubbings***

**Objective:** To explore texture and color using crayons

**Curriculum Connection:** art

**Materials:** old embossed holiday cards, crayons, typing paper

**Preparation:** Place old cards and typing paper in a Christmas Card Rubbings folder. In addition provide an example of a rubbing using a couple of different colors.

**Directions:** Students place the typing paper over the card and rub the crayon lightly over it.

# Lift the Gift

**Directions:** Name the opposite of the word shown on each gift. Lift the flaps to check your answers.

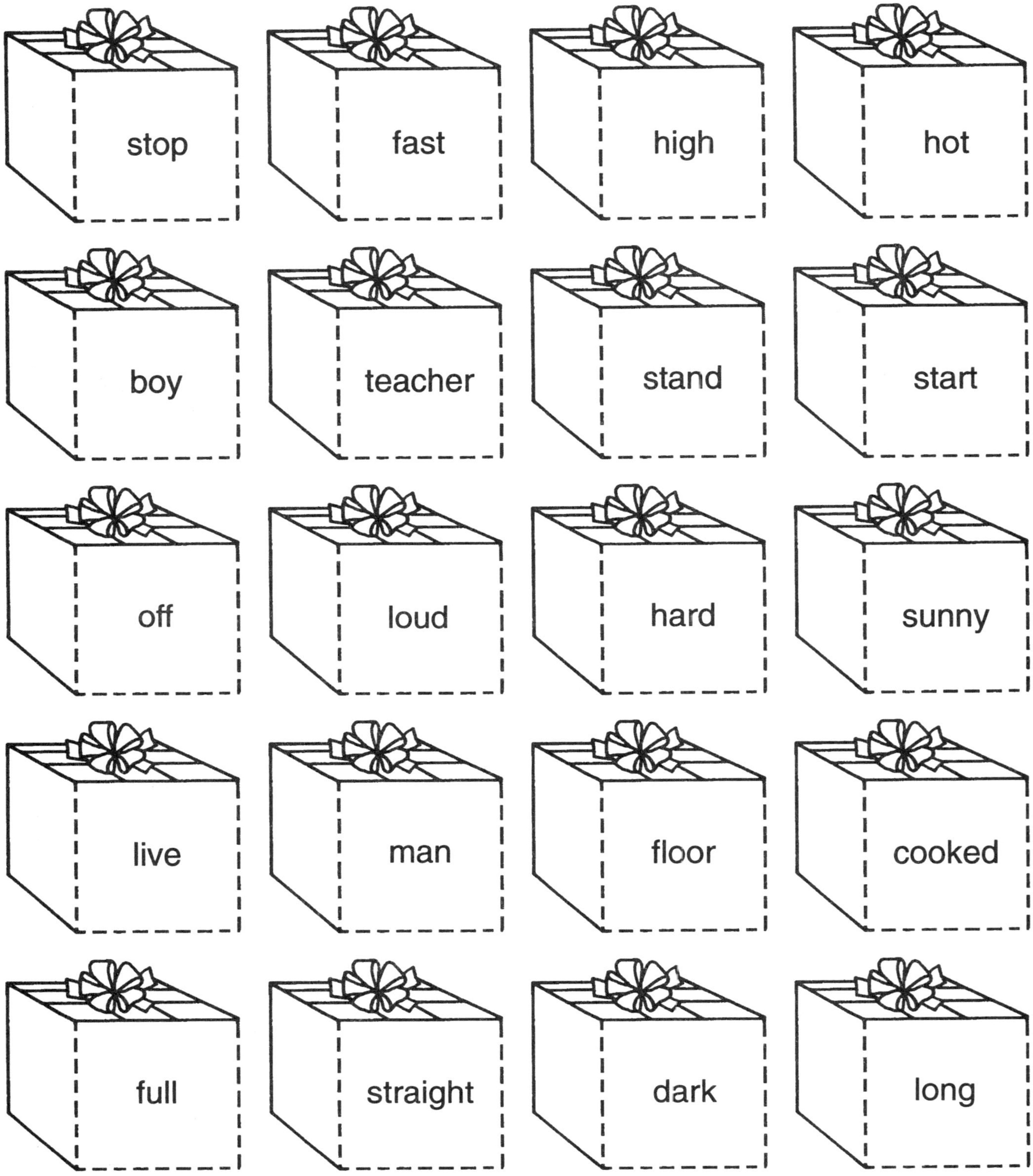


 

# Lift the Gift *(cont.)*

| | | | |
|---|---|---|---|
| go | slow | low | cold |
| girl | student | sit | finish |
| on | quiet | soft | rainy |
| die | women | ceiling | raw |
| empty | curved | light | short |

# Christmas Wrap Around the World

(Front side of wrapping card.)

| | |
|---|---|
| English | Joyeux Noël |
| French | Feliz Navidad |
| German | God Jul |
| Swedish | Merry Christmas |
| Spanish | Kala Christougenna |
| Russian | Fröhliche Weihnachten |
| Greek | Sheng Dan Kuai Le |
| Chinese | S Rozhdestvom Kristovym |
| Japanese | Buon Natale |
| Portuguese | Meri Kurisumasu |
| Italian | Boas Festas |

(Back side of wrapping card.)

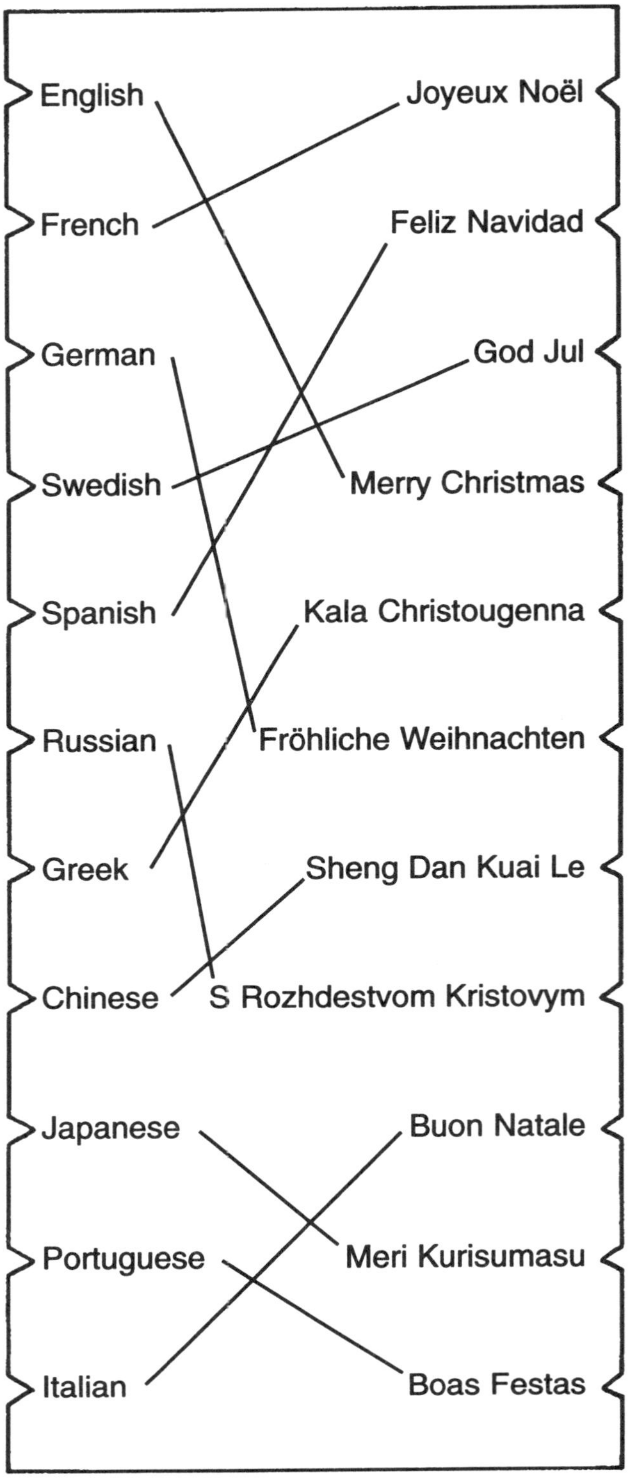


 

# Christmas Poet-Tree

**Directions:** Put the word cards on the tree to make a poem about a Christmas tree.

# Christmas Poet-Tree Word Cards

| | | | | |
|---|---|---|---|---|
| evergreen | star | green | tall | fir |
| pine | branches | angel | string | lights |
| bright | ornaments | silver | gold | gifts |
| presents | wrapped | dangle | hang | top |
| decorated | and | the | with | of |
| under | boughs | colorful | | |

 

# Christmas Gift List

**Directions:** The best gifts are often those that do not cost anything. List some things that you would like to do as a gift for someone, and list some things you would like to have done for you.

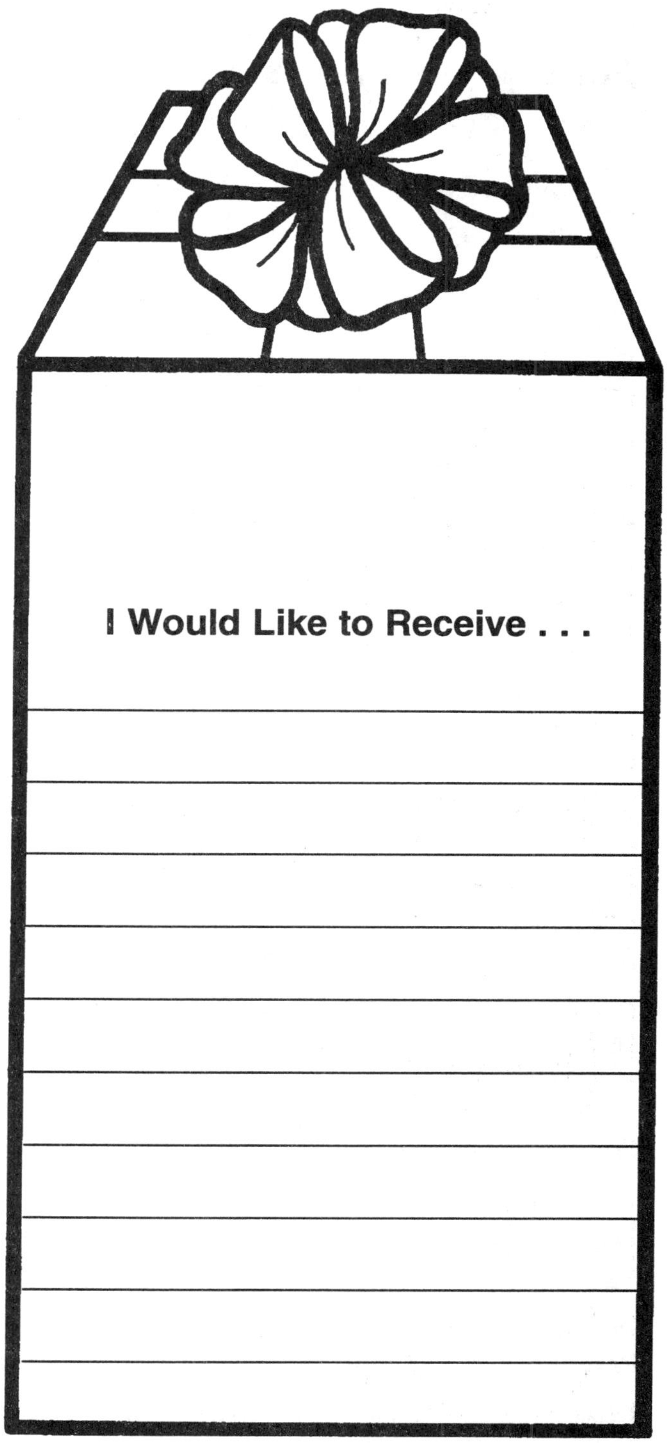

# Kwanzaa

## Background

The uniquely African-American cultural holiday of Kwanzaa is celebrated between December 26th and January 1st. Kwanzaa, which means "first fruits of the harvest," was developed by Dr. Maulana Karenga in 1966 and has seven principles for daily living: unity, self-determination, collective work and responsibility, cooperative economics, purpose, creativity, and faith. Important symbols that relate specifically to the seven principles are fruits and vegetables, woven place mats, a candle holder with seven candles (black, red, and green), ears of corn symbolizing the children in the home, gifts, and a communal unity cup.

## Setting Up the Center

Prepare a Kwanzaa sign. Using the clip art on page 11 color, laminate, and post it in the center.

- ***Surprise Box***

a candle, a cup, a small ear of corn

- ***Suggested Books***

  *Celebrating Kwanzaa* by Diane Hoyt-Goldsmith (Holiday House, 1993)
  *Kwanzaa* by A.P. Porter (Carolrhoda Books, 1991)
  *Seven Candles for Kwanzaa* by Andrea Davis Pinkney (Dial, 1993)

- ***Technology Resource***

*Kwanzaa.* (Video); 10 min. Pied Piper/AIMS Multimedia, 9710 De Soto Ave., Chatsworth, CA 91311; 1-800-367-2567.

## Center Activities

- ***Kwanzaa Mat Weaving***

**Objectives:** To create a Kwanzaa place mat; to promote cultural awareness

**Curriculum Connections:** art, social studies

**Materials:** Kwanzaa Mat (page 41), one per student; green or red construction paper; 1" (2.5 cm) strips of black, green, and red construction paper; scissors

**Preparation:** Reproduce the Kwanzaa Mat on green or red construction paper. Cut the strips of colored construction paper. Fold the mats and strips in half so they can be placed in a Kwanzaa Mat folder. Prepare a partially completed mat and put it in the folder for students to examine.

**Directions:** Students will cut out the mat shape and cut along the dotted lines. They will weave the colored strips into the mat using any pattern they desire.

- ***Traditional African Clothing***

**Objectives:** To acquaint students with traditional African dress; to promote cultural awareness

**Curriculum Connections:** social studies, art

**Materials:** Traditional African Clothing (page 42), one copy per student; Paper Dolls (page 43); scissors; colored pencils, markers, or crayons

**Preparation:** Reproduce the paper dolls on tagboard. Laminate the dolls, then cut them out. Reproduce the clothing patterns for each student and place in a Paper Dolls folder.

**Directions:** Students will color their own sets of traditional African clothes for the paper dolls.

# Kwanzaa Mat

**Directions:** Cut out the mat shape. Carefully cut along the dotted lines. Weave the colored strips into the mat. You can place the colored strips in any order that you like.

# Traditional African Clothing

**Directions:** Color the clothes in any way that you like. Carefully cut out the clothes. Put the clothes on the paper dolls.

# Paper Dolls

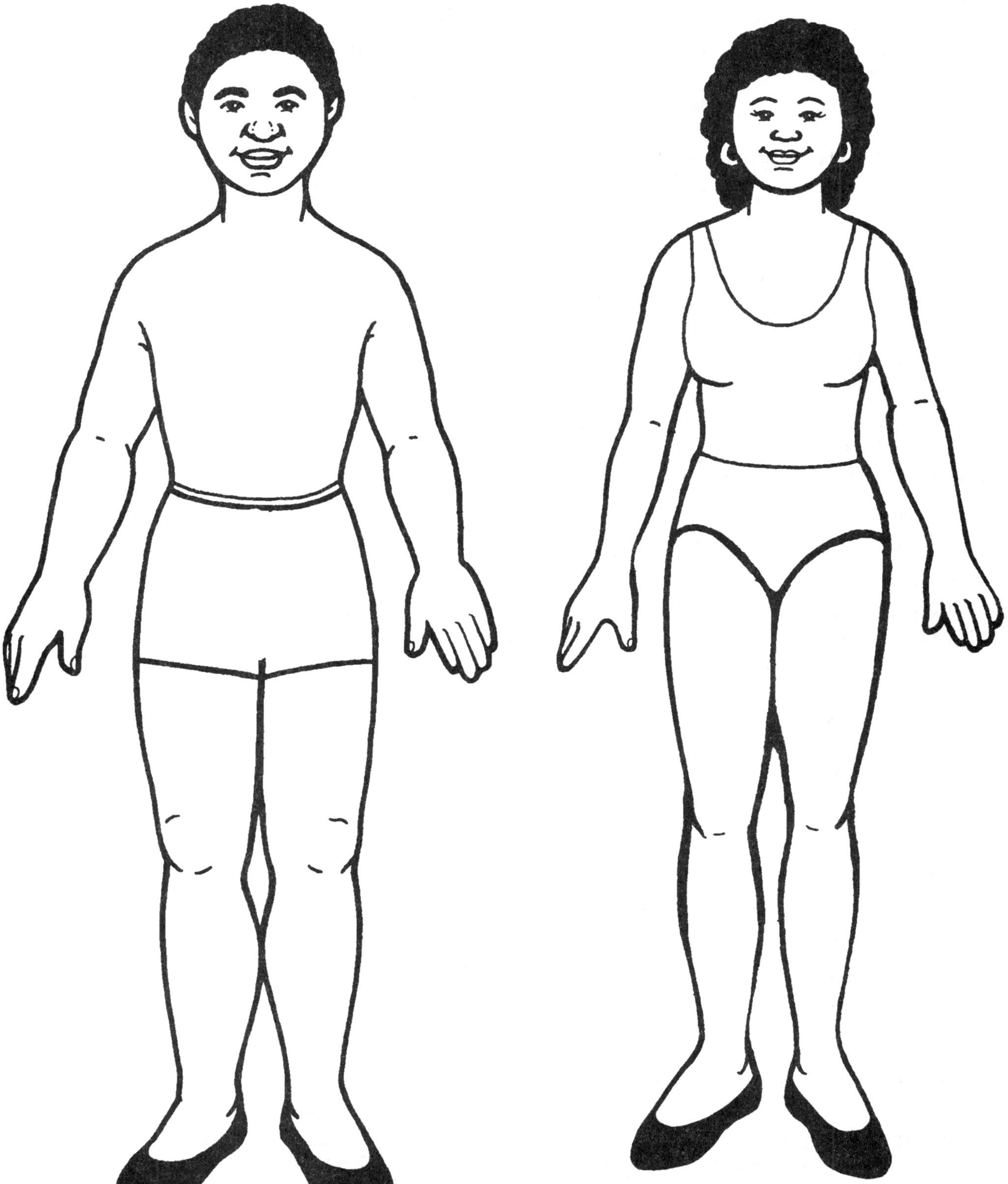

# New Year's

## Background

New Year's Eve is on December 31, and New Year's Day is on January 1. Customs for this holiday come from all over the world and from many different eras: singing "Auld Lang Syne" comes from Scotland, drinking a toast is from the early Anglo-Saxons, making lots of noise comes from the Danes, and watching the lighted ball drop from Times Square in New York City is a uniquely American tradition. Many people consider New Year's a time to make resolutions about things that they want to improve on during the coming year. It is a time of new beginnings.

## Setting Up the Center

Prepare a *New Year's sign.* Color; laminate; and post it in the center.

- ***Surprise Box***

inexpensive plastic watch, egg timer, party noisemaker

- ***Suggested Books***

  *Good Bye Old Year, Hello New Year* by Frank Modell (Greenwillow Books, 1984)
  *Happy New Year* by Emily Kelley (Lerner, 1986)
  *Happy New Year, Beni!* by Jane Breskin Zalben (Holt, 1993)

## Center Activities

- ***Baby New Year's New Beginnings***

**Objective:** To write new goals for the new year

**Curriculum Connection:** language arts

**Materials:** Baby New Year's New Beginnings (page 45), one per student

**Preparation:** Reproduce page 45. Place the copies in a New Beginnings folder.

**Directions:** Students tell or show what they want to learn about or improve upon for the new year.

- ***New Year's Noisemaker***

**Objective:** To create a noisemaker

**Curriculum Connection:** music

**Materials:** toilet paper tube, one per student; hole punch; wax paper, 3" (8 cm) square per student; rubber band, one per student; colored markers

**Preparation:** Display a sample noisemaker. Put the remaining tubes in a bag under the table. Wax paper squares and rubber bands can go in a New Year's Noisemaker folder.

**Directions:** Each student will color and punch holes in a tube and attach the wax paper to one end with a rubber band. Invite students to experiment with their noisemakers.

- ***Father Time's Contractions***

**Objective:** To practice combining words to make contractions

**Curriculum Connection:** language arts

**Materials:** Father Time's Contractions (page 46), scissors, construction paper, glue

**Preparation:** Reproduce page 46 on construction paper, and laminate it. Cut apart the word cards, and place them in the appropriate boxes. Place the activity in a Father Time's Contractions folder.

**Directions:** Students will determine the two words used to make each contraction.

# Baby New Year's New Beginnings

**Directions:** Baby New Year helps us to begin each new year by showing us that we can start all over again. Is there something you would like to learn this year? Is there something you would like to be able to do better? (Here are some ideas: learning a new sport or hobby, having a better attitude at home or school, improving habits like cleaning your room.) Write a paragraph or draw a picture of your new beginning on the scroll shown below.

# Father Time's Contractions

**Directions:** Find the two words that go together to make each contraction then match them to the contractions. The words may be used more than once.

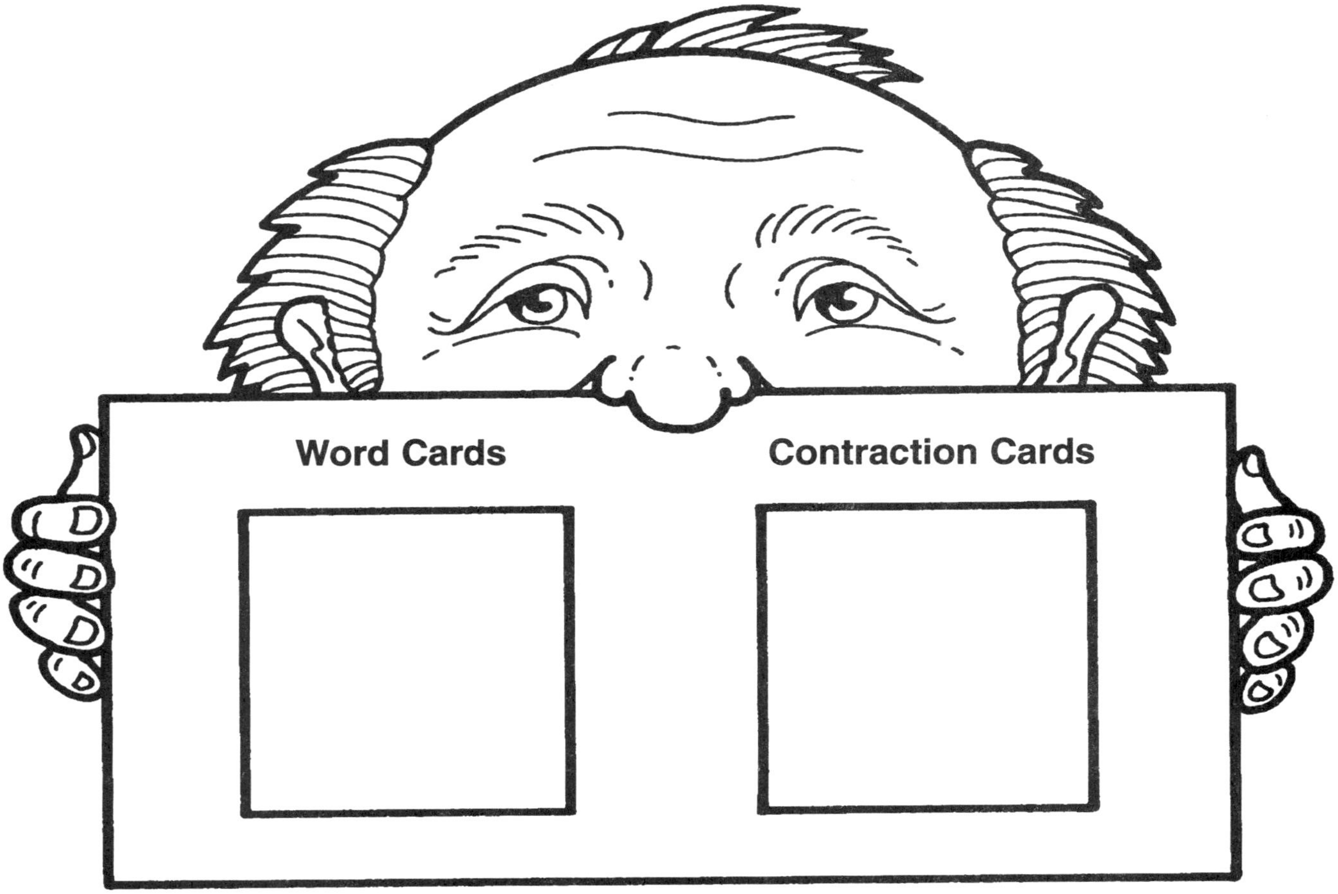


| | | | |
|---|---|---|---|
| can | not | can't | do |
| don't | will | won't | I |
| am | I'm | I'll | it |
| is | it's | there | there's |
| have | I've | they | they've |

 

# Martin Luther King, Jr. Day

## Background

January 15, 1929, is the birthday of African-American hero Dr. Martin Luther King, Jr. He was an educated man, influenced by the writings of Mahatma Gandhi and Henry David Thoreau, who emphasized nonviolent protest as a way to bring about social change. Dr. King worked hard to end the injustice of racial segregation through a variety of nonviolent activities. He organized a city-wide boycott of the buses in Montgomery, Alabama, to protest the law that required African Americans to sit in the back. Dr. King gave many moving speeches, his most memorable being the "I Have a Dream" speech given at the March on Washington in 1963. On April 4, 1968, the country mourned when Martin Luther King, Jr., was assassinated. Today Martin Luther King, Jr. Day is celebrated on the third Monday in January.

## Setting Up the Center

Use the clip art (page 11) to prepare a *Martin Luther King, Jr.* Day sign. Color, laminate, and post it in the center. Provide an audio tape of Martin Luther King's famous "I Have a Dream" speech. Display photographs of Martin Luther King, Jr. or the March on Washington.

- ***Surprise Box***

plastic dove, 1960s peace sign

- ***Suggested Books***

  *Martin Luther King Day* by Lois Lowery (Carolrhoda, 1987)
  *Martin Luther King Day* by Janet McDonnell (Childrens Press, 1993)
  *A Picture Book of Martin Luther King, Jr,.* by David A. Adler (Holiday House, 1989)

- ***Technology Resource***

*Young Martin Luther King, Jr., "I Have a Dream."* (Cassette and 4 paperbacks); Troll Associates, Catalog Sales Dept., 100 Corporate Dr., Mahwah, NJ 07498; 1-800-929-8765.

## Center Activities

- ***"I Have a Dream" Mobile***

**Objective:** To develop a vision for school, family, and self

**Curriculum Connection:** social studies

**Materials:** "I Have a Dream" Mobile (pages 48-49); white construction paper, one piece per student; scissors; colored pencils or markers; hole punch; string, three 8" (0.9 cm) pieces per student

**Preparation:** Reproduce the mobile on construction paper and cut the string. Place these in an "I Have a Dream" Mobile folder. Make a sample mobile to hang from the ceiling above the center.

**Directions:** Students will write or draw their "dreams" for the school, their families, and themselves and hang them from the portrait of Martin Luther King, Jr.

- ***Martin Luther King, Jr. Puzzle***

**Objective:** To put together a puzzle using critical thinking skills

**Curriculum Connection:** math

**Materials:** Martin Luther King Puzzle (page 50), tagboard, glue stick, scissors

**Preparation:** Glue the puzzle onto tagboard, laminate it, and cut along the lines. Put the pieces in a Martin Luther King Puzzle folder.

**Directions:** Students will put the pieces together to make the picture of Martin Luther King, Jr.

# "I Have a Dream" Mobile

**Directions:** Cut out the picture of Dr. King, the "I Have a Dream" strip, and the three dream cards. Write a dream on each card. Put the mobile together as shown.

Dr. Martin Luther King, Jr.

## "I Have a Dream"

# "I Have a Dream" Mobile *(cont.)*

School

Family

Myself

# Martin Luther King, Jr. Puzzle

# Valentine's Day

## Background

February 14 is known as the day of love. Although this holiday has been celebrated for centuries, its origin is unknown. One legend says it started with a Christian martyr named Valentine, who, before his execution, sent a letter to his love and signed it "Your Valentine." Symbols associated with this romantic holiday include hearts, arrows, and chubby cupids. Valentine's Day is a celebration of love and friendship, and people of all ages enjoy sending cards, candy, and small gifts to loved ones.

## Setting Up the Center

Use the clip art (page 12) to prepare a *Valentine's Day* sign. Color, laminate, and post it in the center. Decorate the center with empty heart-shaped candy boxes.

- ***Surprise Box***

small heart-shaped candy box, lace doily, a Valentine; Provide a variety of romantic music, such as Nat King Cole, Italian opera, and/or classical symphony for students to enjoy.

- ***Suggested Books***

  You may wish to place love poems and books about love and friendship in the center.
  *Arthur's Great Big Valentine* by Lillian Hoban (Harper Trophy, 1989)
  *Arthur's Valentine* by Marc Brown (Little, Brown & Co., 1980)
  *Best Friends* by Steven Kellogg (Dial, 1985)
  *Best Friend for Frances* by Russell Hoban (Harper & Row, 1969)
  *It's Valentine's Day* by Jack Prelutsky (Scholastic, 1983)

- ***Technology Resources***

*Cranberry Valentine.* (Filmstrip and cassette; video); 11 min. Pied Piper/AIMS Multimedia, 9710 De Soto Ave., Chatsworth, CA 91311; 1-800-367-2567.

*Little Mouse's Big Valentine.* (Video); 10 min. SRA, P.O. Box 543, Blacklick, OH 43004; 1-800-843-8855.

*A Valentine Mystery.* (Video); 5 min. Troll Associates, Catalog Sales Dept., 100 Corporate Dr., Mahwah, NJ 07498; 1-800-929-8765.

*Valentine's Day Grump.* (Video); 8 min. Troll Associates, Catalog Sales Dept., 100 Corporate Dr., Mahwah, NJ 07498; 1-800-929-8765.

## Center Activities

- ***Very Valentines***

**Objectives:** To encourage creativity; to enhance fine-motor skills

**Curriculum Connection:** art

**Materials:** construction paper (pink, red, white), tissue paper, doilies, lace remnants, glitter, sequins, heart stencils, heart cookie cutters

**Preparation:** Put the construction paper in a Very Valentines folder. Place the other items in plastic resealable bags and put these in a supply basket on the center table.

**Directions:** Students create their own Valentines. Encourage them to be creative.

# Valentine's Day *(cont.)*

## Center Activities *(cont.)*

- ***Conversation Hearts Graph***

**Objectives:** To practice sorting, counting, adding, subtracting, organizing, and graphing

**Curriculum Connection:** math

**Materials:** Conversation Hearts Graph (page 53); small resealable plastic bags filled with 20 candy conversation hearts, one bag per student

**Preparation:** Glue the graph onto tagboard and laminate it. Place the bags with the candy in a plastic basket on the center table.

**Directions:** Each student sorts a bag of candies by color. Students should line up the candies by color on the graph. Then they can use a separate piece of paper to answer the questions shown at the bottom of the graph. When they are finished they can eat their candies.

**Options:** Have younger students write the number of candies in each color group. After everyone has completed the graph, students can answer the questions as a class activity. You may wish to label each bag with a student's name, or hand out the bags as each student goes to the center for this activity.

- ***Pencil Toppers***

**Objectives:** To encourage creativity; to develop fine-motor skills

**Curriculum Connection:** art

**Materials:** Pencil Toppers (page 54), at least one per student on white tagboard; hole punch; crayons or markers; glitter; sequins; glue

**Directions:** Students can color and decorate the pencil toppers and then cut them out. Show them how to use the hole punch to make the holes for the pencil to fit through. These make great student gifts.

- ***Broken Hearts Compound Words***

**Objective:** To practice combining words to make compound words

**Curriculum Connection:** language arts

**Materials:** Broken Hearts Compound Words (page 55), one copy on red or pink construction paper and one copy on white copier paper; scissors

**Preparation:** Reproduce the Broken Hearts Compound Words on a piece of red or pink construction paper and laminate it. Cut out the hearts along the broken lines and put them in a resealable plastic bag. Place the bag in a Broken Hearts folder. For an answer key make a second copy of the Broken Hearts Compound Words on white copier paper and tape it to the inside of the Broken Hearts folder. Write or glue the directions on the outside of the folder.

**Directions:** The student arranges the pieces of the hearts together to make compound words. Self-checking can be accomplished by looking at the answer key inside the folder. There are two blank hearts that can be used to make additional compound words.

**Option:** You may wish to have students put the matched hearts in alphabetical order. The answers are listed that way on the key so students can check themselves.

# Conversation Hearts Graph

**Directions:** Group your candies by color. Line them up by color on the graph. Then answer the questions at the bottom of the page.

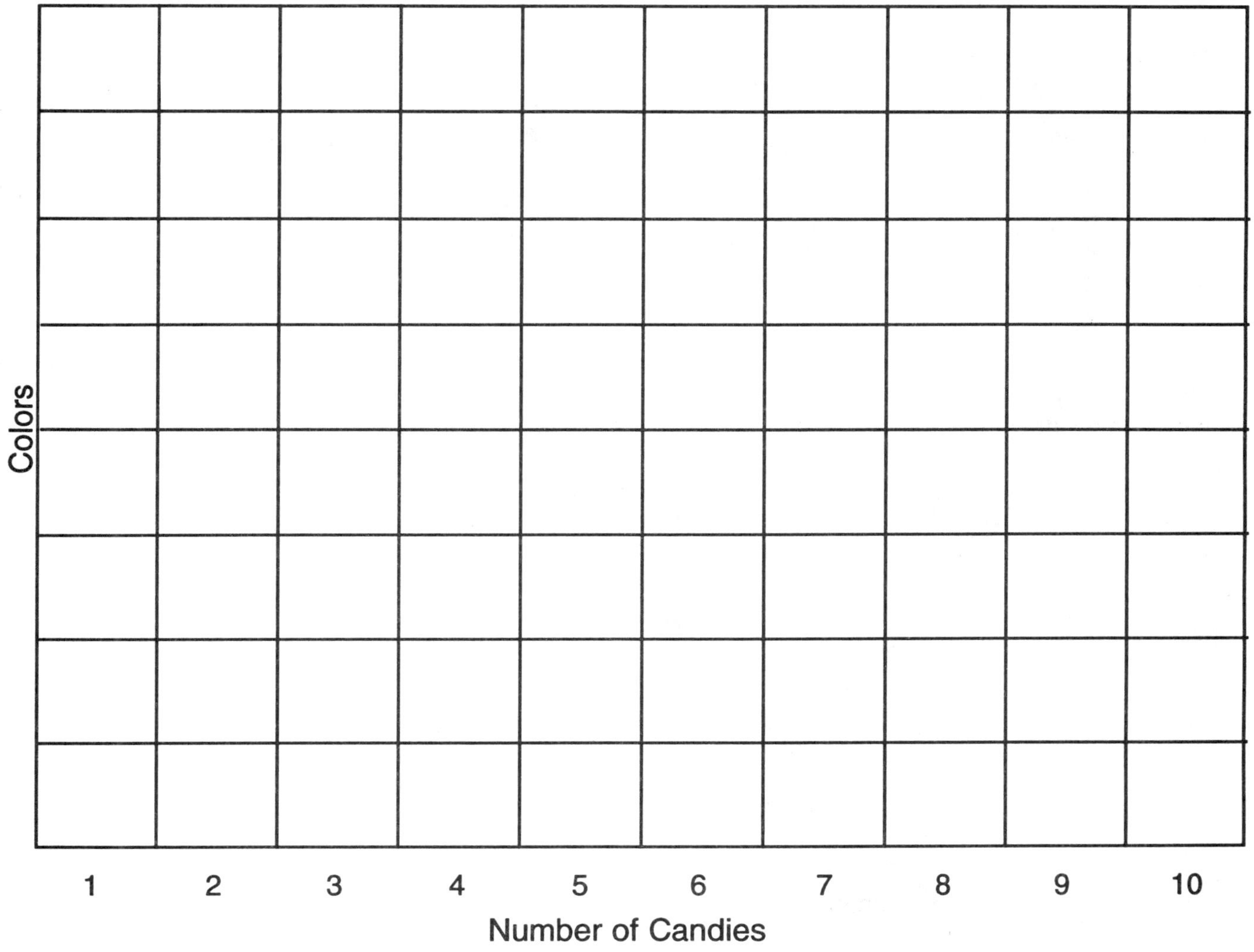


1. Which color has the most candies? ____________
2. How many candies are there in the line that has the most?____________
3. Which color has the fewest candies?____________
4. How many candies are there in the line that has the fewest?____________
5. How many more candies are there for the answer to question 2 than for the answer to question 4?____________
6. (Number of white candies) + (Number of green candies) =____________
7. (Number of candies for the answer to question 2) + ____________.
   (Number of candies for the answer to question 4) =____________.

# Pencil Toppers

**Directions:** Color, decorate, and cut out these pencil toppers. Use a hole punch to make the holes. Slide a pencil through each set of holes.

# Broken Hearts Compound Words

**Directions:** Make compound words by matching the pieces of the broken hearts.

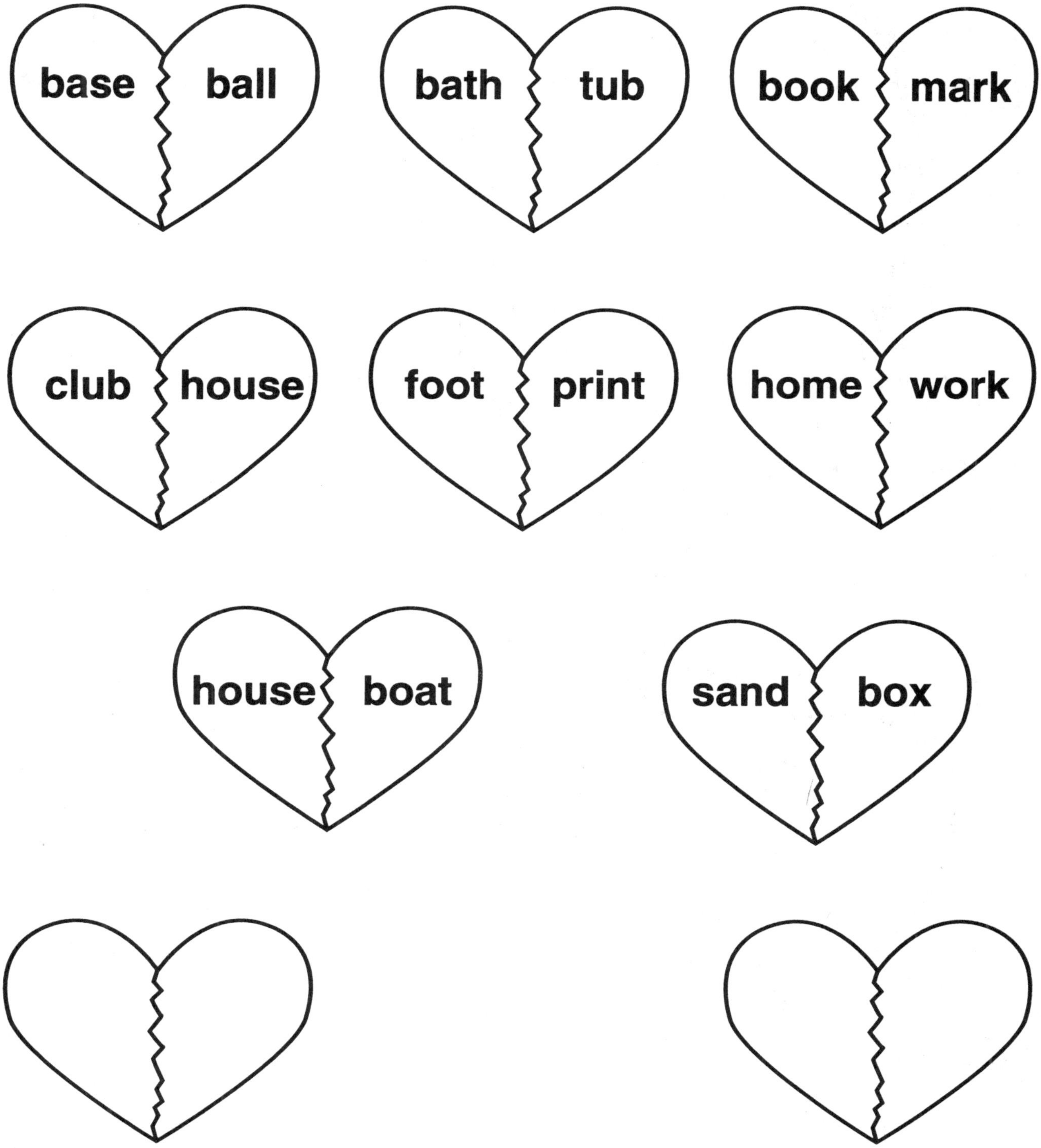

# St. Patrick's Day

## Background

March 17 is the day people of Irish descent, as well as many others, celebrate St. Patrick's Day. St. Patrick is the patron saint of Ireland and is known for bringing Christianity, as well as literacy, to the Irish people. He was well loved and all of Ireland mourned his death on March 17, 493. The color green, shamrocks, jigs, leprechauns, and potatoes are traditional parts of St. Patrick's Day celebrations. Many cities enjoy the day with parades and "wearin' of the green."

## Setting Up the Center

Use the clip art (page 11) to prepare a *St. Patrick's Day* sign. Color, laminate, and post it in the center. Provide a tape of traditional Irish songs and jig music for students to enjoy.

- ***Surprise Box***

chocolate or plastic coins, small Irish flag, shamrock-shaped cookie cutter, live shamrock or clover (to be changed frequently)

- ***Suggested Books***

  *Clever Tom and the Leprechaun* by Linda Shute (Scholastic, 1989)
  *Fin M'eoul, the Giant of Knockmany Hill* by Tomie dePaola (Holiday, 1981)
  *Jamie O'Rourke and the Big Potato* by Tomie dePaola (Putnam, 1992)
  *Patrick, Patron Saint of Ireland* by Tomie dePaola (Holiday, 1992)

## Center Activities

- ***Leprechaun Hand Puppet***

**Objectives:** To create a hand puppet; to promote cultural awareness

**Curriculum Connection:** art

**Materials:** Leprechaun Hand Puppet (page 58), one per student; small paper bag, one per student; green, yellow, and black crayons or markers; green paper strips; glue stick

**Preparation:** Reproduce the Leprechaun Hand Puppet pattern on white copier paper. Put the patterns and paper bags in a Leprechaun Hand Puppet folder. You may wish to prepare a hand puppet as a sample and display it in the center.

**Directions:** Students color their patterns and cut out the pieces. They glue the face to the bottom of the paper bag and the body to the long part of the paper bag. After fan-folding green strips of paper, students should add these to the sides of the bags for the arms.

- ***Leprechaun Maze***

**Objectives:** To practice pre-writing skills; To use critical thinking skills; to promote cultural awareness

**Curriculum Connection:** language arts, handwriting

**Materials:** Leprechaun Maze (page 59), pencils

**Preparation:** Reproduce the Leprechaun Maze. Place the copies in a Leprechaun Maze folder.

**Directions:** Students will help the leprechaun find his pot of gold. They may color the sheet when they are finished.

**Option:** Instead of making one per student, you can make a master copy and laminate it. Students can practice their pre-writing skills by tracing the maze pattern with their fingers or using a dry erase pens.

# St. Patrick's Day *(cont.)*

## Center Activities *(cont.)*

- ***Pot-O'-Gold***

**Objectives:** To practice math skills in a story problem format; to promote cultural awareness

**Curriculum Connection:** math

**Materials:** pot pattern (shown below), black and yellow construction paper, stapler, coin patterns (shown below)

**Preparation:** Enlarge the pot and coin patterns. Trace the pot pattern four times on black construction paper. Cut out the patterns. Staple two patterns together, leaving the tops open, to make two pots. Trace the coin pattern on yellow construction paper, and cut out the coins. Write a question on one side of each coin and the answer on the back. Place all the pieces in a resealable plastic bag in a Pot-O'-Gold folder.

**Directions:** Two students play at a time. They place all of the coins between them. Taking turns, they pick a coin and answer the math question. If the first student gets it correct, he or she puts the coin in his or her pot. If the answer is incorrect, the second student gets a chance. If the answer is correct he or she puts the coin in his or her pot. After all of the coins have been used, students count the number of coins in their pots to see who has the most.

**Option:** For younger students, have play money available as manipulatives to work the problems.

**Pot Pattern**

**Coin Pattern**

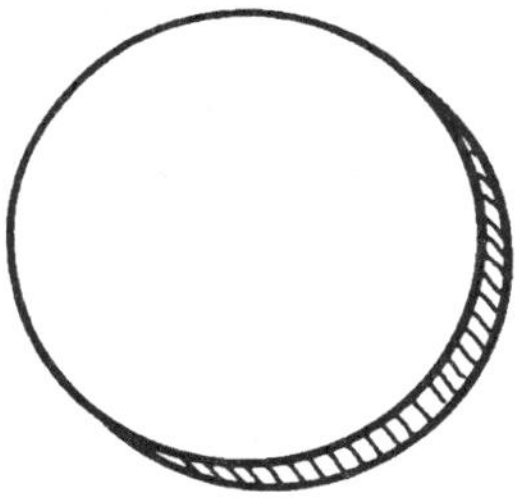

## Coin Questions

A leprechaun with four coins found three more. How many does he have?

A leprechaun with a hole in his pocket lost three of his six coins. How many does he have?

A leprechaun went for a walk and found two coins next to three different trees. How many did he find?

One leprechaun had five coins and his friend had three. How many did they have altogether?

One leprechaun had seven coins. His friend had three. The first one gave some to his friend so that they both had the same number. How many did the leprechaun give away?

A leprechaun with two coins found two more. How many does he have now?

Three leprechauns have the same number of coins. Together they have nine. How many does each leprechaun have?

A leprechaun with four coins borrowed four more. How many does he have now?

A leprechaun with two coins found a pot at the end of the rainbow with eight coins. How many does he have now?

Two leprechauns have three coins each. How many do they have altogether?

# Leprechaun Hand Puppet

**Directions:** Color, cut out, and glue the leprechaun's face and body onto a paper bag. Glue on accordian-folded green paper strips for the arms.

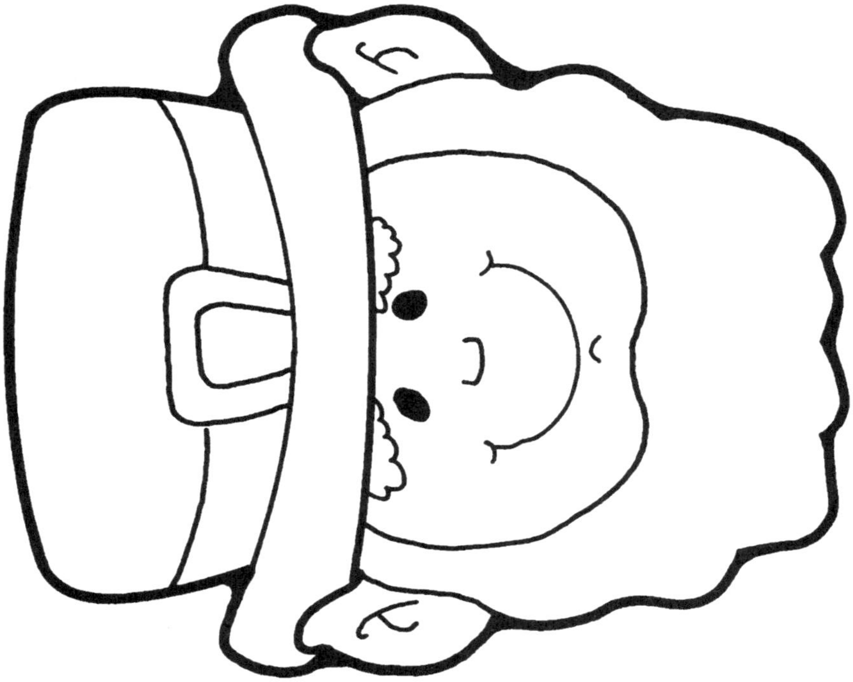

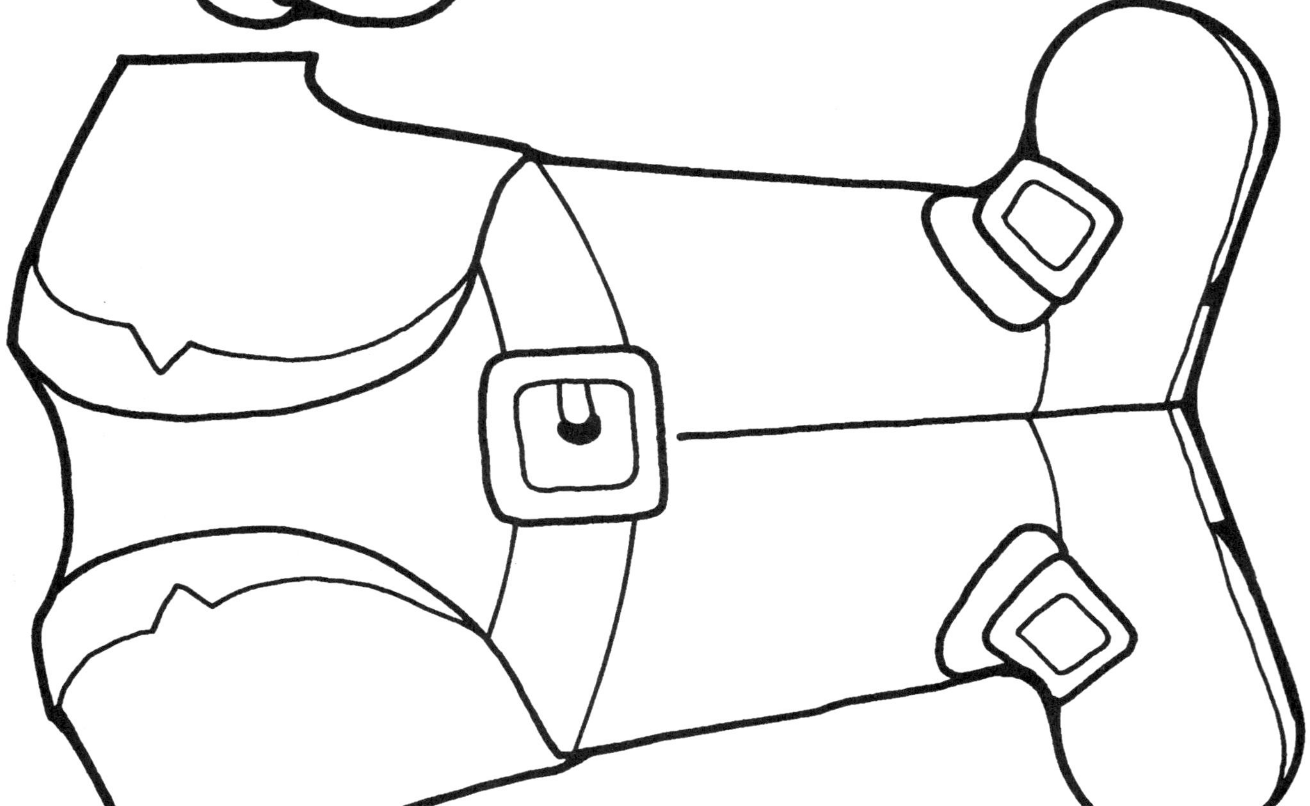

 

# Leprechaun Maze

**Directions:** Help the leprechaun find the pot of gold.

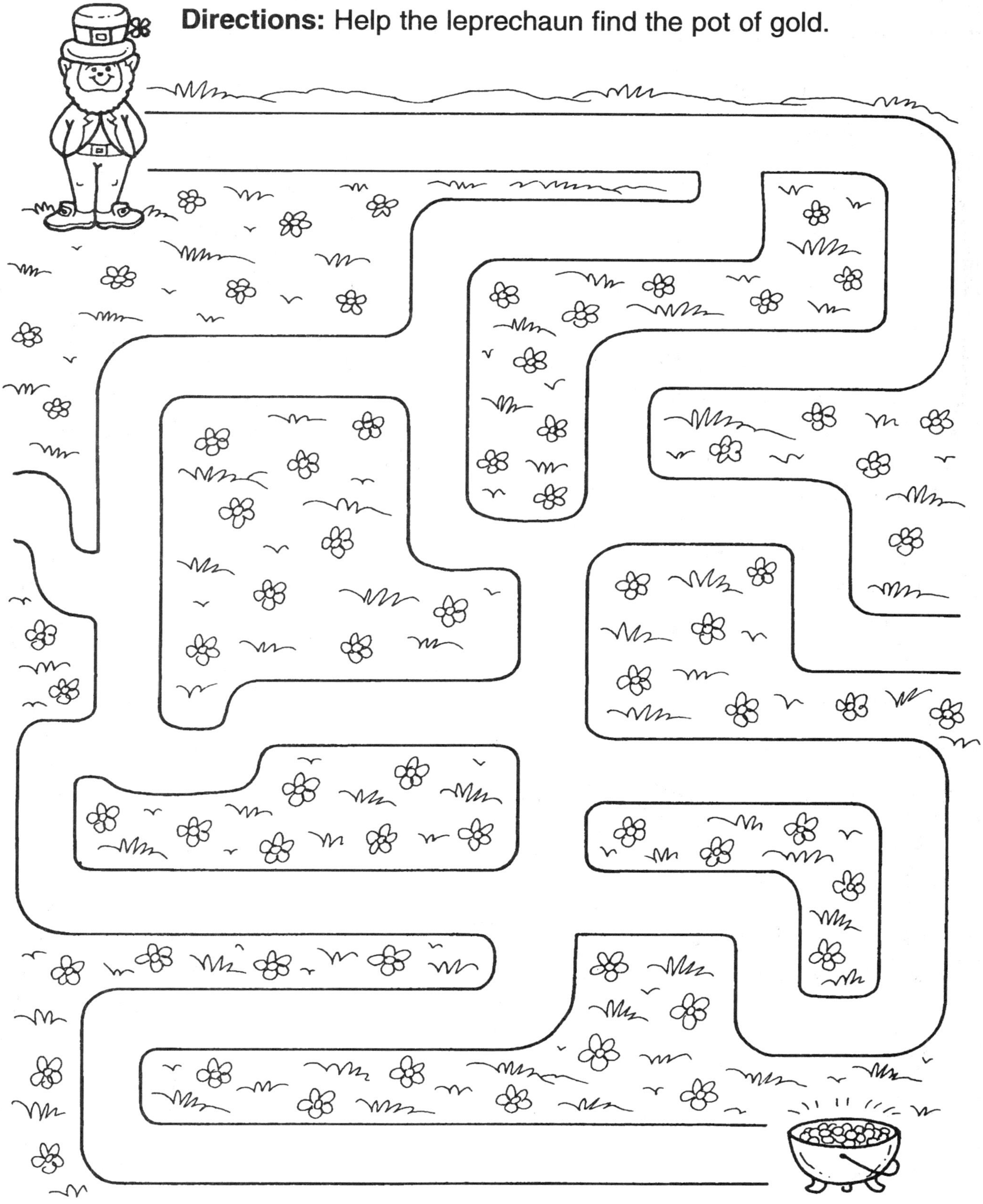

# Easter

## Background

Easter is celebrated between March 22 and April 21 on the first Sunday after the first full moon of spring, signaling the arrival of this season. Easter is a warm and joyful holiday for many reasons. It is one of the holiest days in the Christian calendar, commemorating the resurrection of Jesus Christ a tenent upon which the entire Christian faith is built. In more recent times, Easter has become a springtime celebration centering on the Easter Bunny, coloring and hunting for Easter eggs, and newborn chicks and bunnies.

## Setting Up the Center

Use the clip art (page 12) to prepare an *Easter* sign. Color, laminate, and post it in the center.

- ***Surprise Box***

hard-boiled egg or a plastic egg, small foiled-covered chocolate bunny, small stuffed animal like a chick or bunny, a few pieces of cellophane Easter grass

- ***Suggested Books***

  *The Bunny Who Found Easter* by Charlotte Zolotow (Houghton Mifflin, 1984)
  *The Easter Story* by Brian Wildsmith (Alfred A. Knopf, 1993)
  *The Golden Egg Book* by Margaret Wise Brown (Golden Press, 1947)
  *Humbug Rabbit* by Lorna Balian (Abingdon Press, 1985)
  *Rechenka's Eggs* by Patricia Polacco (Philomel Books, 1988)

- ***Technology Resources***

*Cranberry Easter.* (Filmstrip and cassette); 11 min. Pied Piper/AIMS Multimedia, 9710 De Soto Ave., Chatsworth, CA 91311; 1-800-367-2567.

*Happy Easter.* (Filmstrip and cassette); 7 min. Pied Piper/AIMS Multimedia, 9710 De Soto Ave., Chatsworth, CA 91311; 1-800-367-2567.

*The Great Big Especially Beautiful Easter Egg.* (Video); 9 min. SRA, P.O. Box 543, Blacklick, OH 43004; 1-800-843-8855.

## Center Activities

- ***Jelly Bean Cards***

**Objective:** To practice simple math equations in a game setting

**Curriculum Connection:** math

**Materials:** Jelly Bean Cards (page 62), small bag of jelly beans, addition and/or subtraction flash cards with answers ranging from 1 to 10

**Preparation:** Reproduce page 62 on heavy paper. Laminate and cut out the cards. Put the Jelly Bean Cards and the flash cards in a resealable plastic bag and place them in a Jelly Bean Cards folder. Put 30 or more jelly beans in a resealable plastic bag at the center and refill as necessary.

**Directions:** Three students can play, with one being the caller and the other two answering the equations. The caller picks one flash card at a time and reads the equation but not the answer. The players get the correct answer, then they can check their cards for that number. If it is there, they can put a jelly bean on that space. The winner is the first player to get five jelly beans in a row—horizontally, vertically, or diagonally.

**Option:** For younger students, use the jelly beans as manipulatives to figure out the equations, as well as markers for the game.

## Center Activities (cont.)

- ***Scrambled Spelling Eggs***

**Objective:** To practice spelling skills

**Curriculum Connection:** language arts

**Materials:** plastic Easter eggs, paper, scissors, pen

**Preparation:** Use this as an opportunity to review the previous week's spelling words. Write each word on a slip of paper and cut between each letter. Put all of the letters for one word in each plastic egg. Put the eggs in an Easter basket.

**Directions:** Students unscramble the letters to make a spelling word.

**Option:** For younger students or for unfamiliar words, tape the whole word on the outside of the egg. Then students can match the scrambled letters with the word shown on the egg.

- ***Eggheads***

**Objective:** To plant and grow seeds

**Curriculum Connection:** science

**Materials:** egg shells, cleaned with bleach, one half shell per student; potting soil; spoons; grass seed; permanent marking pens; empty egg cartons; sponge for clean-up; small spray bottle with water

**Preparation:** Stack the egg shells upside down. Make an egghead of yourself as a sample.

**Directions:** Each student uses the permanent marking pen to carefully draw his/her face on the egg shell half (be sure the shell has the open part on top before drawing.) Then the student spoons potting soil into it until it is three-quarters full. A few grass seeds are sprinkled on top and sprayed lightly with water. Students should keep the eggs on upside down egg cartons until they are taken home. Students should be sure to clean up.

- ***Jelly Bean Estimation***

**Objective:** To practice estimating skills

**Curriculum Connection:** math

**Materials:** jar filled with jelly beans, empty cube-shaped tissue box, small pieces of scratch paper

**Preparation:** Fill a small jar with jelly beans. Older students can use a larger jar. Use the empty tissue box for students' estimates.

**Directions:** Students estimate how many jelly beans are in the jar. They write their estimates on scratch paper and place them in the tissue box. Have the class help you count the jelly beans. You may also wish to have students sort the jelly beans. The student who guesses the closest to the actual number of candies gets to keep the jar.

- ***Ukrainian Egg Designs***

**Objective:** To decorate an egg; to promote cultural awareness

**Curriculum Connections:** art and social studies

**Materials:** Ukrainian Egg Designs (page 63), one or two per student; white construction paper; crayons or markers

**Preparation:** Reproduce the egg designs on white construction paper. Cut the pages in half. Place the egg design in a Ukrainian Egg Designs folder. Write or glue the directions on the outside of the folder.

**Directions:** Students color the egg designs.

# Jelly Bean Cards

**Directions:** Use jelly beans to cover the numbers on your Jelly Bean Cards.

**Jelly Beans**

| J | E | L | L | Y |
|---|---|---|---|---|
| 7 | 6 | 4 | 5 | 3 |
| 9 | 7 | 9 | 1 | 6 |
| 5 | 2 | Free | 7 | 4 |
| 6 | 9 | 7 | 2 | 9 |
| 10 | 4 | 5 | 3 | 8 |

**Jelly Beans**

| B | E | A | N | S |
|---|---|---|---|---|
| 10 | 7 | 6 | 2 | 3 |
| 5 | 4 | 5 | 7 | 4 |
| 7 | 10 | Free | 4 | 6 |
| 1 | 5 | 9 | 8 | 7 |
| 9 | 9 | 3 | 1 | 8 |

# Ukrainian Egg Designs

**Directions:** Color the egg.

**Directions:** Color the egg.

# Earth Day

## Background

Earth Day, celebrated on April 22, was started in the 1960s as an attempt to educate people about the need to take care of the Earth's resources. Air and water pollution are major concerns, and today people focus on recycling as a means of re-using our resources instead of destroying more of nature. Recycling is especially relevant to school age children since it is something they can easily do.

## Setting Up the Center

Use the clip art (page 12) to prepare an *Earth Day* sign. Color, laminate, and post it in the center.

- ***Surprise Box***

crumpled up fast food wrapper, Styrofoam egg carton section, small toy can or plastic bottle

- ***Suggested Books***

  *Dear World: How Children Around the World Feel About the Environment* ed. by Lannis Temple (Random House, 1993)

  *Earth and I* by Frank Asch (HBJ, 1994)

  *Earth and the Sky* by Jean-Pierre Verdet (Scholastic, 1992)

  *Earth Day* by Linda Lowery (Carolrhoda Books, 1992)

  *The Earth is Painted Green* by Barbara Brenner (Scholastic, 1994)

  *Keepers of the Earth: Native American Stories and Environmental Activities for Children* by Michael J. Caduto and Joseph Bruchac (Fulcrum, 1989)

  *Recycling* by Joan Kaebacken (Childrens Press, 1991)

  *Tanya's Big Green Dream* by Linda Glaser (Macmillan, 1994)

- ***Technology Resource***

*Holiday Facts and Fun: Earth Day.* (Video); 10 min. Pied Piper/AIMS Multimedia, 9710 De Soto Ave., Chatsworth, CA 91311; 1-800-367-2567.

## Center Activities

- ***Garbage Sorting***

**Objective:** To practice sorting skills

**Curriculum Connection:** math

**Materials:** miscellaneous pieces of clean garbage, a small box

**Preparation:** Collect various clean items that students would usually think of as trash and place them in a small box on the center table. **Warning:** DO NOT USE ANY GLASS OR SHARP METAL OBJECTS; ALL ITEMS MUST BE EMPTY AND CLEAN. Examples include small plastic water bottle, soda can, fast food wrapper, mini cereal box, lid from a jar, plastic jar, milk carton, egg carton sections, potato chip bag, soup can label, prepared potato or rice mix box, rice bag, toilet paper roll, plastic detergent container.

**Directions:** Students sort the garbage into various groups: lids and containers, plastic and cardboard, recyclable and nonrecyclable, food and non-food, etc.

 

# Earth Day *(cont.)*

## Center Activities *(cont.)*

- ***I Can Read That!***

**Objective:** To encourage word recognition skills

**Curriculum Connection:** language arts

**Materials:** bags, boxes, and labels from various foods and prepared mixes; scissors; glue; 8" x 10" (20 cm x 26 cm) pieces of tagboard, one per student

**Preparation:** Cut out the panels from the boxes so that all of the materials can lie flat. Put all of the items in an I Can Read That! folder

**Directions:** Explain to students that you will be recycling product boxes for a reading project. Students will cut out the various brand and product names that they can read to make collages. Even students who cannot "read" will recognize many brand and product names.

**Option:** Encourage students to bring in their own boxes and labels from home. They will be more likely to be able to read things they are familiar with.

- ***Can Cuties***

**Objective:** To recognize that some garbage can be re-used for creative purposes

**Curriculum Connection:** art

**Materials:** empty clean soda cans, spray paint, glue, plastic wiggly eyes, rick-rack, lace, felt scraps, fabric scraps, scissors

**Preparation:** Squash the cans so that they are long and have the bottom pressed onto the top of the can.

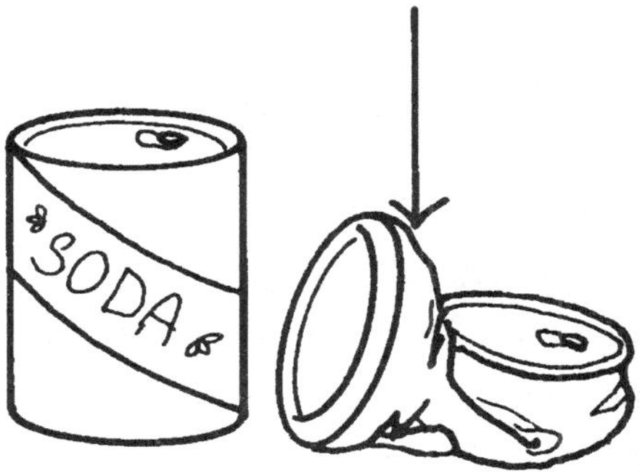


Spray paint all of the cans at one time. Put them in a paper bag under the center table. Put fabric and other craft supplies into a plastic bin on the table.

**Directions:** Students make people out of the cans, using the scraps to create faces and clothing.

**Option:** You could have other small pieces of clean garbage for students to use in their recycled art such as pop tops from the soda cans as earrings.

- ***Helping the Earth***

**Objective:** To increase awareness of how individuals can help the environment

**Curriculum Connections:** science, social studies, art

**Materials:** drawing paper, markers or crayons

**Preparation:** Place the drawing paper in a Helping the Earth folder. Place the crayons or markers in a plastic bin on the table.

**Directions:** Students draw pictures of themselves doing an activity that will help the environment. Examples include collecting newspapers or cans, picking up litter, planting gardens or trees, cleaning graffiti off of walls and other surfaces, and reusing clean food containers.

# Mother's Day

## Background

Many countries and cultures honor mothers with special days. In the United States, Mother's Day is celebrated on the second Sunday in May. On this special day, mothers often receive small gifts, cards, special chores, and breakfast done for them in bed. Some people wear carnations in honor of their mothers—red ones for mothers who are living and white for those who have died.

***Setting Up the Center***

Use the clip art (page 12) to prepare a *Mother's Day* sign. Color, laminate, and post it in the center.

- ***Surprise Box***

a silk or plastic flower, a spatula, a hair bow, a clip-on earring

- ***Suggested Books***

  *Are You My Mother?* by P.D. Eastman (Random House, 1960)
  *Blueberries for Sal* by Robert McClosky (Viking Press, 1948)
  *Happy Mother's Day* by Steven Kroll (Holiday House, 1985)
  *Happy Mother's Day!* by Deborah Hautzig (Random, 1989)
  *Is Your Mama a Llama?* by Deborah Guarino (Scholastic, 1989)
  *Love You Forever* by Robert Munsch (Firefly Books, 1986)
  *Make Way for Ducklings* by Robert McClosky (Viking Press, 1941)
  *Mama, Do You Love Me?* by Barbara M. Joosse (Scholastic, 1991)
  *Mama's Secret* by Maria Polushkin (Four Winds, 1984)
  *Mother's Day* by Wilma Willis Gore (Enslow, 1993)
  *Mother's Day Mice* by Eve Bunting (Houghton Mifflin, 1986)

## Center Activities

- ***Mom's Mini-Book***

**Objective:** To create a book telling why mothers are appreciated

**Curriculum Connection:** language arts

**Materials:** Mom's Mini-Book (page 67), scissors, crayons or markers, stapler

**Preparation:** Reproduce the Mom's Mini-Book and place in a Mom's Mini-Book folder.

**Directions:** Students cut and staple the pages to make mini-books. They fill in the blanks to tell about their mothers and draw pictures to show the things that they have written about.

- ***Mother's Day Card***

**Objective:** To create a card for Mother's Day

**Curriculum Connection:** art

**Materials:** construction paper, wallpaper and wrapping paper scraps, scissors, glue stick

**Preparation:** Fold pieces of construction paper in half to make the cards. Write the word Mom in large outlined letters on a half-sheet of paper. Reproduce it. Put the copies and the folded construction paper in a Mother's Day Card folder.

**Directions:** Students decorate the word *Mom* with the wrapping paper and wallpaper scraps. Then they glue it to the outside of the folded construction paper. Inside the cards, students should draw themselves with their mothers.

 

# Mom's Mini-Book

**Directions:** Cut apart the pages of the mini-book. Fill in the blanks to tell about your mother. Draw a picture for each page. Staple the pages together to make your mini-book.

My mom is GREAT!

1

My mom loves to

________________________________ .

________________________________

2

When I am at school all day, my mom ________________________________ .

________________________________

3

I love it when my mom

________________________________ .

________________________________

4

# Father's Day

## Background

Father's Day is a special day set aside to honor fathers. On this day, children give their fathers cards and gifts and treat them in special ways. It is thought that this holiday started in June of 1910, thanks to a Mrs. John B. Dodd, who wanted to honor her father for his dedication to raising her and her five siblings after their mother's death. Father's Day is a special time for families and a good reminder for children to honor the fathers or father figures in their lives.

## Setting up the Center

Use the clip art (page 12) to prepare a *Father's Day* sign. Color, laminate, and post it in the center.

- ***Surprise Box***

paintbrush, empty or toy razor, large belt buckle, baseball, metal toy car, tie

- ***Suggested Books***

  *50 Below Zero* by Robert Munsch (Annick Press, 1986)
  *Daddies* by Adele Aron Greenspun (Philomel, 1991)

## Center Activities

- ***Tie Patterns***

**Objective:** To create stripe patterns

**Curriculum Connection:** math

**Materials:** Tie Patterns (page 69), one per student; 2-4 different colored markers

**Preparation:** Reproduce Tie Patterns and place the copies in a Tie Pattern folder.

**Directions:** Students decorate their ties with color patterns that they choose.

**Options:** For younger students, make a couple of tie patterns for students to copy.

- ***Dad Word Strip***

**Objective:** To practice phonics skills

**Curriculum Connection:** language arts

**Materials:** Dad's Word Strip (page 70); colored construction paper (multicultural construction paper, if available); scissors; craft knife

**Preparation:** Reproduce Dad's Word Strip on multicultural or colored construction paper. Laminate the copies for durability. Cut off the letter strips. Cut slits in the mouth, so the strip can slide through it.

**Directions:** Students slide the strip through the mouth and sound out "-ad" words.

- ***Dad's Doings***

**Objective:** To practice critical thinking skills by analyzing which items go together

**Curriculum Connection:** language arts

**Materials:** Dad's Doing (page 71); scissors; colored markers, optional

**Preparation:** Reproduce Dad's Doings. Tape a completed copy inside of a Dad's Doings folder as an answer key.

**Directions:** Students draw lines to match the items that belong together.

# Tie Patterns

**Directions:** Choose a pattern of colors for each tie. Then color the ties using your patterns.

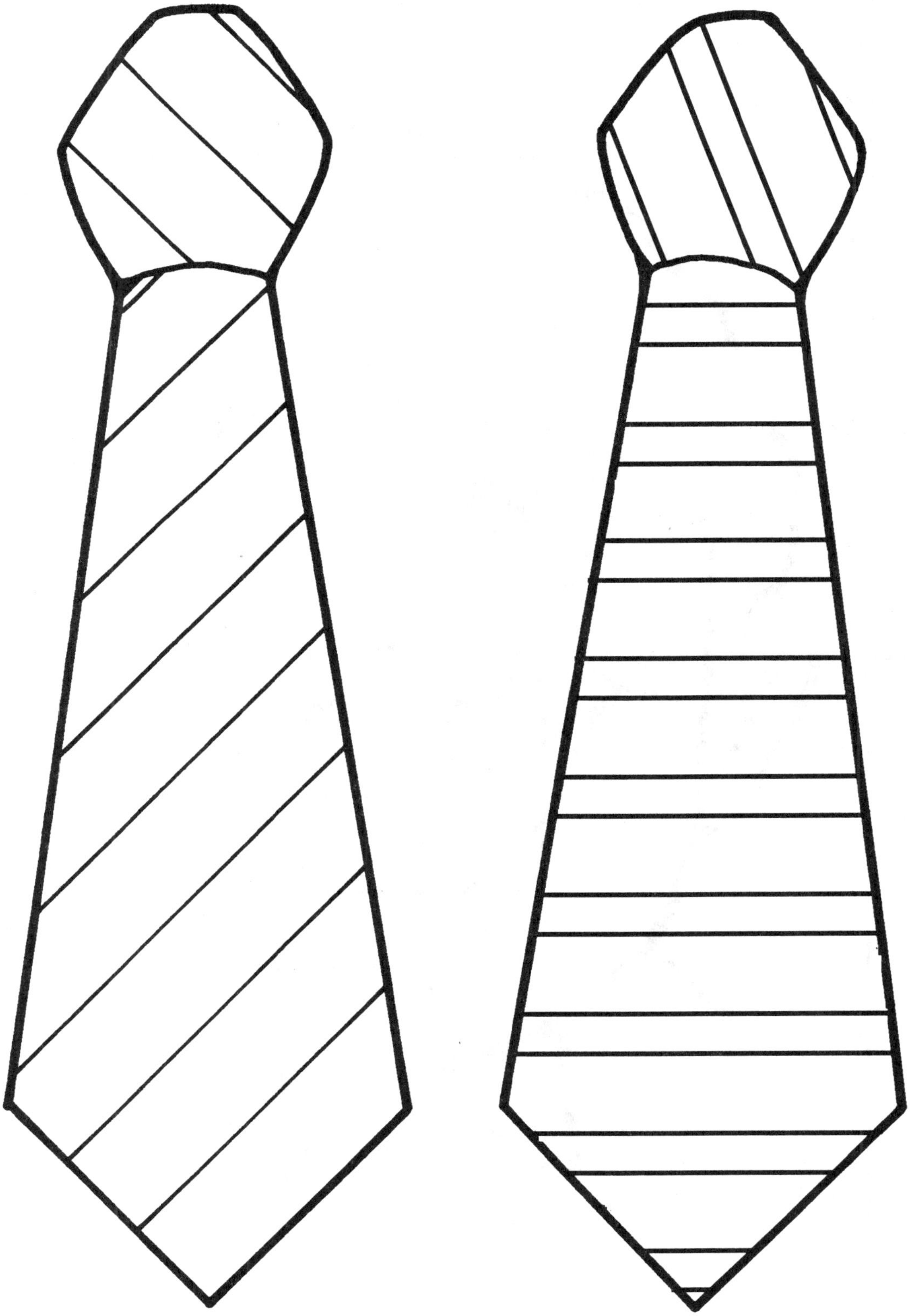

# Dad Word Strip

**Directions:** Slide the letter strips through Dad's mouth. Read the words that you make.

| |
|---|
| d |
| b |
| f |
| h |
| l |
| m |
| p |

| |
|---|
| d |
| s |
| t |
| br |
| gl |
| cl |
| r |

# Dad's Doings

**Directions:** Dads enjoy doing many different types of activities. Draw lines to match the items that go together.

# Patriotic/National Holidays

Depending on which country, state, or province you live in, you will want to select some of the following holidays to supplement the other major holidays you have chosen for your center. Some of the activities suggested will be appropriate for many of the different holidays.

- ***COLUMBUS DAY*** ***(October 12th)***

**Background:** Columbus Day, or "Dia de la Raza" ("Day of the Race") in Canada and Latin America, is a day to celebrate the historic journey and accomplishments of Christopher Columbus who discovered the New World on October 12, opening North America to a number of explorers and settlers. Since Columbus' trip was sponsored by Spain, you may also wish to have students discuss the contributions made by Spaniards to our culture and the rest of the world.

**Setting Up the Center:** Prepare a *Columbus Day* sign. Display books in the center that tell about explorers, including space explorers.

**Center Activities:** Have students write a journal page as if they were explorers in Be an Explorer (page 75). They can write about or draw pictures of somewhere they would like to explore, real or imaginary, or they can pretend to be Columbus and write about exploration in the late 1400s.

- ***ELECTION DAY*** ***(First Tuesday in November)***

**Background:** Every republic or democratic country has a day set aside for selecting their government officials.

**Setting Up the Center:** Use the clip art (page 12) to prepare an *Election Day* sign. Display books about Election Day, voting, and presidents. You can also hang or post old election materials, such as buttons, fliers, posters, and bumper stickers, to add to the patriotic flavor of Election Day.

**Center Activities:** Have students make buttons either for class elections or for current national/local political elections with the patterns on page 76. Put construction paper buttons in an Election Day Buttons folder. Use two-sided tape or safety pins to attach them to students.

- ***VETERANS DAY*** ***(November 11th)***

**Background:** Veterans Day, which is also called Remembrance Day in Canada and England, was originally named Armistice Day to commemorate the anniversary of the day on which the Allies and Central Powers signed the agreement ending The Great War (World War I). Since that time many wars have been fought, so the name was changed to honor all of those who have served their countries by being in the armed forces. People often take wreaths to the grave sites of deceased veterans on this day.

**Setting Up the Center:** Use the clip art (page 12) to prepare a Veterans Day sign. The Surprise Box can contain a small fabric flag or an armed forces pin or medal. **Warning:** Be sure to cover any exposed points of the pin or medal with tape or glue.

**Center Activities:** Students can make patriotic wreaths using small grapevine or Styrofoam wreaths that are available at craft stores. They can decorate the wreaths with small flags and red, white, and blue ribbons and sequins. Students can give the wreaths to veterans they know, or the class can deliver them to a nearby veterans' hospital. Also, students can decorate the medals on page 76. Cut out the circles and put them in a Veterans Day Medals file. Students can glue them onto clean lids from frozen orange juice cans and add ribbons to the medals.

 

# Patriotic/National Holidays *(cont.)*

- ***PRESIDENTS' DAY*** ***(Third Monday in February)***

**Background:** Some states celebrate George Washington and Abraham Lincoln's birthdays separately, while others unite them as Presidents' Day. George Washington, who is called "the Father of our country," was a farmer, soldier, and the first president of America. His birthday is on February 22nd. Abraham Lincoln, whose birthday is on February 12th, was perhaps the second most influential president in United States history. He is known for trying to preserve the unity of the states and freeing the slaves during the Civil War. Because both Washington and Lincoln exhibited admirable qualities and played significant roles in the history of the United States, they are the only two presidents who are honored with holidays on their birthdays.

**Setting Up the Center:** Use the clip art (page 11) to prepare a *Presidents' Day* sign. For the Surprise Box, include a birthday candle, a penny, and a quarter.

**Center Activities:** Students can do rubbings of the coins that have Lincoln and Washington on the front sides (penny and quarter). If possible, provide copper and silver colored crayons for the rubbings. Older students can count the values of their rubbed coins. Challenge them to make certain values such as 22 cents, 56 cents, one dollar, etc. Reproduce page 78 and place the activity in a Money Matching folder. Students match the presidents' heads with the money on which they appear. Make two copies of the Do You Know Your Presidents? game (page 77). Tape one copy in a Do You Know Your Presidents? folder as an answer key. Glue the other copy onto construction paper, laminate it, and cut out the sentence strips. Place the strips inside the folder. Write or glue the directions on the outside of the folder.

- ***CINCO DE MAYO*** ***(May 5th)***

**Background:** The fifth of May is a special day for Mexicans and Mexican Americans. This holiday commemorates the Mexican victory over the well-equipped French army in 1862. Parades, piñatas, and mariachi bands are common ways to celebrate.

**Setting Up the Center:** Prepare a *Cinco de Mayo* sign. Display books in the center that are about Hispanics or the Hispanic culture.

**Center Activities:** Reproduce page 79. Tape one copy inside a Cinco de Mayo folder as an answer key. Glue another copy onto construction paper, laminate it, and cut out the squares. Students match the pictures with the Spanish number words.

- ***MEMORIAL DAY*** ***(May 30th or the last Monday in May)***

**Background:** This special day honors those individuals in the United States who have died while serving in the military. Parades and special ceremonies take place to honor these heroes. Because Memorial Day is so close to the end of the traditional school year, it is often considered the unofficial start of the summer season.

**Setting Up the Center:** Use the clip art (page 12) to prepare a *Memorial Day* sign. If possible, provide tapes of patriotic music and songs, especially music by John Phillip Sousa, for students to enjoy.

**Center Activities:** Make medals as described for Veterans Day (page 72) and flags as described for Flag Day (page 74).

# Patriotic/National Holidays *(cont.)*

• ***FLAG DAY (June 14th)***

**Background:** The United States flag has changed many times since the Continental Congress first passed a resolution in 1777 stating that America's flag would consist of 13 red and white stripes and 13 stars on a blue square. In 1818 a law was passed that the flag would have 13 stripes and one star for each state that was added to the Union.

**Setting Up the Center:** Use the clip art (page 12) to prepare a *Flag Day* sign. Also hang United States flags—cloth, postcards, photographs, illustrations, etc.—to show the flag in as many ways as possible.

**Center Activities:** Have students put together the pieces to make United States flags. In a Flag Day folder, put 8½" x 11" (22 cm x 28 cm) sheets of white construction paper (one per student), one-inch (2.5 cm) wide strips of red construction paper, 4" x 4" (10.5 cm x 10.5 cm) blue squares, and small star stickers. Students can assemble their own American flags.

• ***CANADA DAY (July 1st)***

**Background:** Canada Day, or Dominion Day, is the day that Canadians celebrate as their Independence Day. It was on July 1, 1867, that the British Parliament ruled to have Canada become a territory of Great Britain rather than under its direct rule. Just like Independence Day in the Untied States, the day ends with spectacular fireworks shows.

**For the Center:** Prepare a *Canada Day* sign. If possible, locate a tape that contains the Canadian national anthem. Students will enjoy looking at travel books or *National Geographic* magazines that have photographs of Canada. Display a map of Canada.

**Center Activities:** Make Glittery Fireworks Art by watering down glue in a bottle. Each student drips a puddle of glue on a piece of heavy paper and blows on it with a straw. After the glue spreads, the student sprinkles on colored glitter. Prepare some examples ahead of time and display them in the center. Students can also make Canadian flags with red rectangles on either side of a piece of white construction paper. Have them paste or trace real maple leaves in the centers of their flags.

• ***INDEPENDENCE DAY (July 4th)***

**Background:** The Fourth of July, or Independence Day, is the birthday of the United States of America. It is the anniversary date of the signing of the Declaration of Independence written by Thomas Jefferson and signed by the Continental Congress. This act of defiance against the mother country, England, led to the beginning of the Revolutionary War. Independence Day is celebrated with picnics, family reunions, and fireworks displays in communities across the country.

**Setting Up the Center:** Use the clip art (page 12) to prepare a *Independence Day* sign. Provide tapes of patriotic music and songs, especially music by John Phillips Sousa, for students to enjoy.

**Center Activities:** Make Glittery Fireworks Art as described above for Canada Day. Invite students to make a picture strip showing American landmarks using the song "My Country 'Tis of Thee" (page 80). Students cut out and glue the two strips together. Then they color in the landmarks and symbols of America. Make American flags as described above for Flag Day.

# Be an Explorer

**Directions:** Write about or draw a picture of a real or imaginary place that you would like to explore.

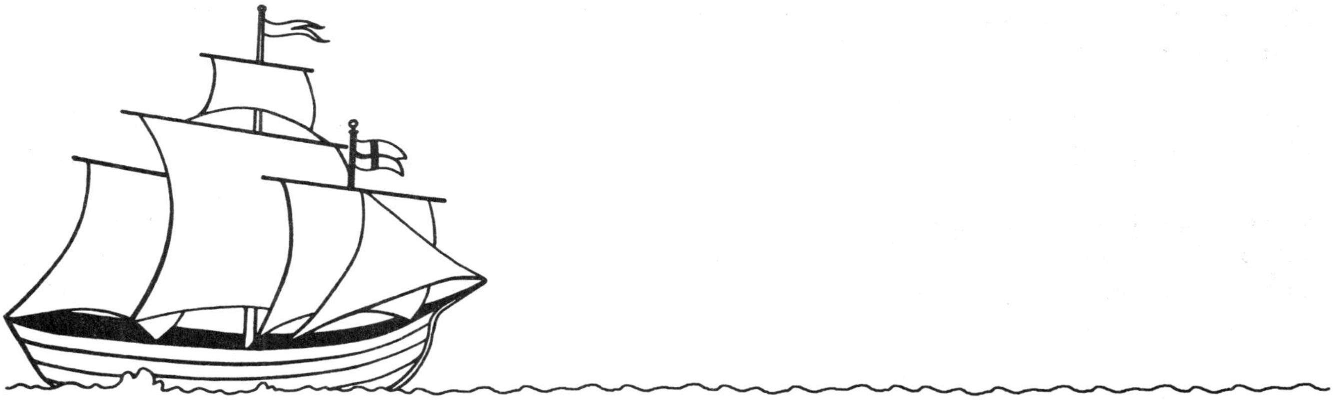

# Buttons and Medals

Voting is
**POWER!**

**Vote for**
________________.

Thank a
**Hero**
Today!

**Medal of**
**Honor**

**Medal of**
**Valor**

# Do You Know Your Presidents?

**Directions:** Read the sentence strips. Separate the statements that are true about George Washington from those that are false. Do the same for Abraham Lincoln.

| **True Statements About George Washington** |
|---|
| He had a wife named Martha. |
| His house had a name—Mount Vernon. |
| His face is on the quarter and the one dollar bill. |
| **False Statements About George Washington** |
| He really wanted to be a king, rather than the first president of America. |
| He was killed during the American Revolution. |
| **True Statements About Abraham Lincoln** |
| He lost many elections before he became president. |
| He grew up in a log cabin, and his home was his school. |
| He was president during the Civil War. |
| **False Statements About Abraham Lincoln** |
| He lived for many years after being shot by John Wilkes Booth. |
| He did not do anything about slavery during the Civil War. |

# Money Matching

**Directions:** Cut out the presidents' heads and glue them to the money on which they appear.

# Spanish Words

**Directions:** Match the pictures with the correct number words.

uno

seis

dos

siete

tres

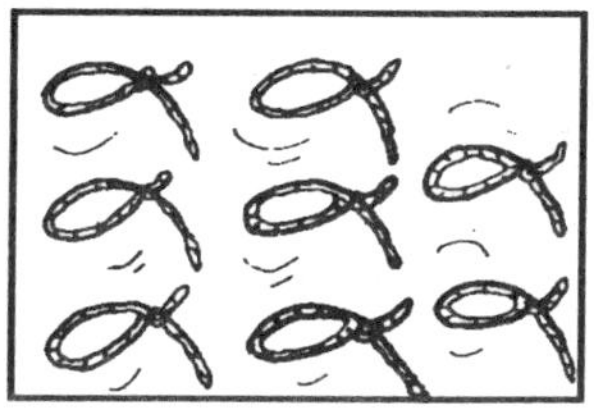

ocho

cuatro

nueve

cinco

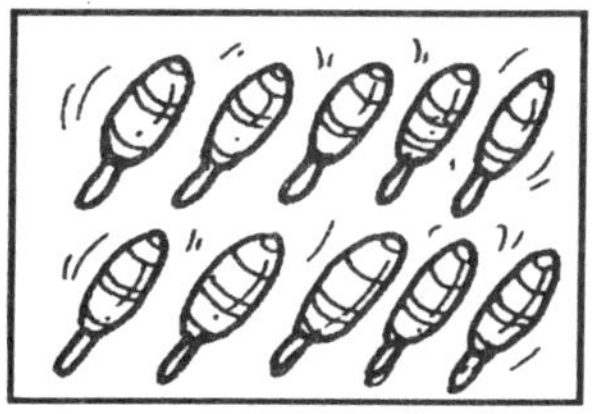

diez

# "My Country 'Tis of Thee"

**Directions:** Cut out the strips. Color the pictures. Glue them together at the tab.

My county tis of thee

1

Sweet land of liberty,
of thee I sing.

2

Land where my
fathers died

3

(tab)

Land of the Pilgrims'
pride

4

From every
mountain side

5

Let freedom ring.

6

 